# Images of War

# TWIN MUSTANG
## THE NORTH AMERICAN F-82 AT WAR

## Alan C. Carey

Pen & Sword
**AVIATION**

First published in Great Britain in 2014
and reprinted in 2020 by
PEN & SWORD AVIATION
an imprint of
Pen & Sword Books Ltd,
47 Church Street,
Barnsley,
South Yorkshire,
S70 2AS

A CIP record for this book is available from the British Library.

ISBN 978 1 78346 221 6

Printed and bound by CPI UK

MIX
Paper from
responsible sources
FSC® C013604

Pen & Sword Books Ltd incorporates the Imprints of
Pen & Sword Aviation, Pen & Sword Maritime,
Pen & Sword Military, Wharncliffe Local History, Pen & Sword Select,
Pen & Sword Military Classics and Leo Cooper.

For a complete list of Pen & Sword titles please contact
Pen & Sword Books Limited
47 Church Street, Barnsley, South Yorkshire, S70 2AS, England

E-mail: enquiries@pen-and-sword.co.uk
Website: www.pen-and-sword.co.uk

# Contents

# Introduction

At the beginning of the Second World War American radar technology and night fighter development was considerably inferior to that of the British. By 1943, however, American technology began to surpass British radar systems with the introduction of the SCR-720. Throughout the Second World War aircraft companies in the United States produced 900 night fighters for the U.S. Army Air Force

**The Northrop P-61 Black Widow, after production delays, began its operational career in Europe in mid-1944 and later in the Pacific. It remained as the Air Force's only night fighter until 1948. (U.S. Air Force)**

(USAAF) while the U.S. Navy and Marine Corps operated a considerably larger number because existing front-line fighters were better suited for adaptation to the night fighter configuration. Late in November 1945, the USAAF approved military characteristics for a jet-propelled aircraft as a post-war successor to the Northrop P-61. At first the all-weather interceptor was conceived as an aircraft that would be effective in daylight as well as at night or during inclement weather. However, by 1946, Major General Curtis LeMay, Deputy Chief of Staff for Research and Development, indicated that this concept be revised due to the added weight of the radar gear which would limit aircraft performance. Because the heavy radar-equipped all-weather fighter would be no match for a small day fighter, 'all-weather' was to mean primarily night and inclement weather. Military performance characteristics were then revised to conform to this decision and designs for two experimental all-weather aircraft, the Curtiss XP-87 Blackhawk and Northrop XP-89 Scorpion, were selected for investigation.

Post-war apathy by the American public and government in the wake of the Second World War cut deeply into military appropriations and stifled night/all-weather fighter development, and the newly established U.S. Air Force (USAF) and the Navy continued to rely on piston-driven night fighter aircraft. Changing international situations in Europe and Asia resuscitated interest in night and all-weather interceptors. Soviet aggression with the establishment of communist-bloc countries of Eastern Europe, the Berlin Crisis of 1948, and the Soviet's testing of a crude nuclear bomb in 1949, forced the U.S. military on a quest to develop superior strategic bombers and jet interceptors, which in turn, resulted in the development of air intercept radar and all-weather aircraft. Early attempts to develop jet-powered all-weather fighters ran into a series of snags and delays. The Air Force ordered the Curtiss XP-87 in December 1945, but it ran into developmental difficulties and the Air Force abandoned the project, which incidentally ended Curtiss' thirty-year history as an aircraft manufacturer. The P-89 Scorpion seemed to hold greater promise, but it too ran into teething troubles and its acceptance and delivery did not occur until 1952.

Development of jet-powered all-weather aircraft would be slow and, until such time when this type became available, the U.S. Air Force needed an interim aircraft. In the immediate post-war period, the P-61 had formed the bulk of the night fighter force. Due to the lack of any suitable jet-powered replacement, the P-61 soldiered

**The U.S. Air Force, in need of a jet-powered all-weather fighter to replace its Second World War P-61 Black Widow, narrowed its search down to the Curtiss XP-87 pictured here and the Northrop XP-89 Scorpion. Ultimately, the underpowered XP-87 lost to the XP-89. (U.S. Air Force)**

on for a few more years. However, manoeuvres held in the North-western United States early in 1948 quickly confirmed the Black Widow's limitations and the Air Force deemed the aircraft as having no tactical value in defensive operations. In order to help fill the gap until the F-89 Scorpion became operational, North American Aviation (NAA) developed a night and all-weather adaptation of the piston-engine North American F-82 Twin Mustang.

Since the P-82, like the P-61, would be of little value in daylight operations, the Air Force assigned such jet interceptors as the Lockheed P-80 Shooting Star (later F-80) and Republic P-84 Thunderjet (F-84) to fighter-interceptor squadrons, which began replacing the single-engined, propeller-driven North American P-51 (F-51) Mustang in the Air Force inventory. These jet aircraft possessed the required speeds to combat enemy bombers of the Boeing B-50 type but both fighters lacked the electronic equipment to allow them to operate at any other time than during daylight (again, the weight of 1950s-era airborne radar technology precluded its use in a small high-speed interceptor). In turn, beginning late in 1949, the North American F-86A Sabre replaced the F-80 and F-84. By the end of 1950, of the 365 aircraft assigned to the U.S. Air Defense Command (ADC), 236 were F-86A and E models. Therefore, without a real all-weather interceptor, the Air Force had no other alternative but to place its reliance on a dual fighter force, with jet aircraft for daytime operations and radar-equipped F-82s for night and inclement weather interceptor missions.

**The Northrop XP-89 Scorpion seemed the answer but continued power plant problems delayed production of the Scorpion forcing the Air Force to rely on modifications of North American Aviation's F-82 Twin Mustang. (*U.S. Air Force*)**

# Chapter One:
# **Development**

Possibly one of the oddest American aircraft to go into full production after the end of the Second World War, the P- (later) F-82 Twin Mustang series was the last mass production propeller-driven fighter acquired by the U.S. Air Force. Originally designed as a long-range bomber escort during the Second World War, it evolved into a night and all-weather fighter during the post-war years. The original concept of the XP-82 traces back to the development of North American Aviation's XP-51 Mustang in 1940 and the production of subsequent variants of that aircraft as a long-range fighter to protect Allied bombers against the German Luftwaffe and, subsequently, to provide cover for Boeing B-29 bombers in the Pacific. However, the Air Force lacked an interceptor with an extreme-range capability. The USAAF fighters with the longest range during that conflict were the P-51D Mustang, with a maximum range of 1,600 miles, and the Lockheed P-38J Lightning with a maximum range of 2,200 miles. Both aircraft were capable of escorting B-17 and B-24 bombers from bases in England to the heart of Germany; but it was another story in the Pacific.

The vast distances of the Pacific, where missions could last eight to twelve hours, required a fighter with a far better range than any existing aircraft in the Air Force's inventory at the time, but such a design would need a two-man crew consisting of a pilot and co-pilot/navigator to reduce workload stress and fatigue. The concept for such a radical aircraft design, closely resembling two P-51 Mustang fighters joined together with a common centre wing and horizontal stabilizer, belonged to Edgar Schmued, North American Design Chief, who proposed the idea in November 1943 at the company's factory in Inglewood, California. Two months later on 7 January 1944, when General of the Army Air Force Hap Arnold was taking a tour of the factory, Ed Schmued showed him the revolutionary design; the General quickly endorsed the project. After viewing a mock-up and wind tunnel model of the design, Air Force brass issued development contract AC-2029 on 8 February 1944 ordering the construction of three experimental prototypes (serial numbers 44-83886 through 44-83888), with the NAA company designation NA-120.

Frontal view of XP-82 scale model about to undergo wind tunnel testing by the National Advisory Committee for Aeronautics (NACA) Ames Research Center during late 1944. (NASA)

# XP-82

North American engineers developed the two airframes and wings for the NA-120 from the basic fuselage and wings of the experimental XP-51F, which was used to develop the P-51H production model. Although the P-51 and XP-82 were quite similar in appearance, very few components were interchangeable. External design changes included lengthening the aft fuselage sections by fifty-seven inches, internal strengthening of the centre and outer wing sections to allow for fuel and armament

**North American's one-quarter scale XP-82 model undergoes testing at in the California Institute of Technology (CalTech) wind tunnel in mid-1944. From the company's model NA-120 proposal, the U.S. Army Air Force originally ordered four prototypes in fact consisting of two XP-82s and two XP-82As. One XP-82A, 44-83888, was constructed powered by Allison V-1710-119 engines: however, it appears that problems with the engines ended further development while the other XP-82A, 44-83889, was cancelled before its construction. (*Nicholas A. Veronico*)**

on external pylons, increasing the length of the ailerons, inclusion of slotted flaps along the trailing edge of the centre section, and enlarging the dual vertical stabilizers to improve stability. Hydraulically operated wing flaps extended from the aileron to the fuselage on each wing panel and between the fuselages on the centre section interconnected and controlled by a lever located in the pilot's cockpit only. Interestingly the XP-82's entire wing area of 408 square feet was less than two Mustangs (470 square feet) but the overall length was six feet longer than the P-51H; a nine-foot difference with the F-82G model. The XP-82 prototypes and the subsequent P-82B variant, used counter-rotating Aeroproducts propellers powered by two liquid-cooled, supercharged, two-stage, two-speed, Packard Merlin V-1650 engines with, on the left (portside), a V-1650-23 and right (starboard), a V-1650-25

**One of the XP-82s under construction at North American Aviation's California plant *circa* early 1945. The fuselages were developed from the company's XP-51F Mustang design. (*Robert F. Dorr*)**

**Both XP-82s, serial numbers 44-83886 and 44-83887, were powered by two V-1650 Packard Merlin engines, the same type engine used in the P-51B Mustang and subsequent models. (*Robert F. Dorr*)**

to compensate for torque. The aircraft's fuel system consisted of four internal self-sealing wing tanks; one consisting of two interconnected cells in each outer wing panel and two in the wing centre section with a total fuel capacity of 575 gallons. This arrangement allowed each engine to operate with a separate and complete fuel system with the two cells interconnected by a cross-feed line. Range and flight time could be increased by the addition of either two 110, 165, or 310-gallon drop tanks installed under each outer wing panel.

The first prototype, serial number 44-83886, rolled out of the Inglewood factory on 25 May 1945 and flew on 16 June 1945, with NAA test pilot Joe Barton and Edward M. Virgin at the controls. This was the second attempt; the month before it refused to get off the ground due to excessive drag caused by the props' air flowing upwards to the centre wing section, an effect created by the rotation of the propellers – the left, counter-clockwise, and the right clockwise. Engineers solved the problem by switching the engines to the opposite sides resulting in successful flight testing. The second prototype, serial number 44-83887, made its initial flight of approximately one hour on 30 August 1945. The first and second prototypes showed the aircraft to have exceptional high speed, manoeuvrability, and rate of climb. The USAAF accepted the first prototype in August 1945 followed by the second the following month. The XP-82 was 39 feet in length with a wing span of nearly 52 feet and its two Merlin engines gave it a top speed of 468 mph, almost identical to the P-51H, and a maximum range of nearly 3,500 miles with internal and external fuel stores (over twice the range of the P-51).

The Twin Mustang's command pilot's port cockpit contained a full set of flight instruments and controls while the co-pilot/navigator position, although equipped

**The second XP-82, 44-83887, poses on North American's ramp at what is now Los Angeles International Airport *circa* 1945. The small spike-like objects near the top of the vertical stabilizer are antennas for the Identification Friend or Foe (IFF) equipment. (*Warren M. Bodie via Robert F. Dorr*)**

XP-82 shows the centre wing and horizontal stabilizer as it banks over the mountains of Southern California. This aircraft was accepted by the Army Air Force in September 1945. (*American Aviation Historical Society*)

**The second XP-82 in flight with a P-51D Mustang serving as chase aircraft during testing over Southern California. Behind the left cockpit is a direction finder loop antenna.** (*San Diego Aerospace Museum via Nicholas A. Veronico*)

with basic instrumentation to fly the aircraft, lacked other features. Both cockpits provided essential power plant and flight controls with the capability to transfer control of guns, fuel, engine heat, anti-icing gear, and the command radio by shift switches in each cockpit. However, the co-pilot had no control over landing gear and flaps (unless in an emergency), or engine ignition, surface control boost, bombs (except salvo), and rockets. In a situation where the command pilot might become incapacitated, NAA equipped both cockpits with an emergency landing gear release handle located at the right side of both cockpits. Pulling the handle unlocked the gear and fairing doors, and actuated a hydraulic pump valve, which allowed trapped hydraulic fluid in the landing gear and wheel door cylinders to return to the system reservoir. This allowed the doors to open and the gear to extend by gravity without hydraulic pressure. North American also included an option for turning the Twin Mustang into a single-seat fighter by removing cockpit equipment from the co-pilot's position, and removing and fairing over the canopy.

The proposed armament package for the XP-82 consisted of a bank of six M-3 .50-caliber machine guns, with 400 rounds-per-gun, housed in the centre wing section. The prototype and subsequent production models allowed for the installation of underwing and centreline racks to carry up to twenty-five 5-inch High Velocity Aircraft Rockets (HVAR), 4,000lbs of bombs – two on each outer wing, two on the centre wing section, or a chemical tank (AN-M10 or AN-M33) which was used to lay smoke screens or dispense chemical agents and was installed on each outer wing rack. North American also provided for an optional removable pod for the centre section that could house eight additional .50-caliber machine guns, radar,

**Cutaway drawing of the first production model as drawn by NAA aviation artist Reynold Brown. The first XP-82 and subsequent production P-82B Twin Mustangs were powered by Packard-Merlin V-1650 engines. (*Nicholas A. Veronico*)**

The XP-82 was rated to carry a total of 6,000lbs of bombs including a 1,000lb bomb on each outer wing pylon and a 2,000lb bomb on each inner pylon. (*Robert F. Dorr*)

120-0-2K

or a photographic reconnaissance package. However, except for the radar pod, the gun pod never materialized for operational aircraft while the photographic reconnaissance package was fitted and tested on only one aircraft. Production models were equipped with the K-18 compensating gun sight installed on the instrument panel shroud of the pilot's cockpit. The sight automatically computed the correct lead angle of fire and consisted of two optical systems, fixed and gyroscopic, contained within the sight. The reticle of the fixed sight, projected on the reflector glass, consisted of a seventy-mil circle with a small cross in the centre, and a rocket scale located below the cross. The fixed sight's circle and cross was used only when strafing, firing rockets, or when the gyro sight malfunctioned. The reticle of the

**Scale model of the XP-82 with removable gun pod prior to wind tunnel testing at the National Advisory Committee for Aeronautics (NACA) Ames Research Center on 3 March 1945. (*NASA*)**

NACA
A-7442
3-3-45

The first XP-82 serial number 44-83886 with the removable gun pod under the centreline containing eight M3 .50 caliber machine guns, which was never used operationally, and intended to supplement the six machine guns located above the pod. (*Norm Taylor Collection via Robert F. Dorr*)

Side view of the .50 calibre gun pod slung beneath the XP-82. NAA also envisioned a 40mm cannon pod but it never went beyond the design stage. (*U.S. Air Force via Nicholas A. Veronico*)

120-61-8 C

Frontal view of the optional detachable gun pod designed by **NAA's** Chief Aerodynamicist Ed Horkey. This would have given the aircraft a devastating amount of firepower. (*U.S. Air Force via Nicholas A. Veronico*)

An **XP-82** with the ordnance that it was capable of carrying, including 500lb bombs and 5-inch **HVAR** rockets under the outer wings, it was also capable of carrying bombs under the centre wing. (*U.S. Air Force*)

gyroscopic sight, also projected on the reflector glass, consisted of a circle with six diamond-shaped images surrounding a central dot. Both sights were used together to automatically compute the lead angle needed to fire on a hostile aircraft.

The Air Force accepted the first prototype on 30 August 1945 but NAA retained it for eighteen months and, after a series of airworthiness and stability flights, it was sent to Wright Field, Ohio, for evaluation by the Air Force's Air Material Command. Afterward, the National Advisory Committee for Aeronautics (NACA) operated it until 1955 when it was scrapped. The Air Force accepted the second prototype on 11 September 1945 and like the first XP-82, NAA kept it for further flight testing until turning back over to the Air Force in March 1946. NACA received it in October 1947, operating it until February 1950 when it sustained major damage after sliding off a runway.

**The second XP-82 shown during ram-jet testing during 1948, was transferred from the newly formed U.S. Air Force to NACA in October 1947. (NASA)**

Rigged for ram-jet engine testing, the second XP-82 prepares for departure from Cleveland, Ohio's Lewis Research Facility during 1948. (*American Aviation Historical Society*)

The second XP-82 with bent props and a twisted fuselage was damaged beyond repair when it ran off an icy runway on 25 February 1950. (NASA)

The first XP-82, serial number 44-83886, was redesignated then transferred to **NACA** in April 1948 and stationed at Langley Field, Virginia. It is seen here during missile testing at the Langley Research Center on 5 May 1951. (*NASA*)

Another view of the first XP-82, designated as NACA 114, taken 1 December 1951 at the Langley Research Center. It was scrapped on 5 October 1955 after accumulating nearly 300 hours of flying time. (*NASA*)

C-28901
12·1·51

# P-82B Model

The USAAF ordered 500 Merlin-powered P-82B Twin Mustangs (Model NA-123) on 8 March 1944 with production contract AC-2384, sixteen months before NAA test pilot George 'Wheaties' Welch took the first P-82B, 44-65160, aloft for the first time on 31 October 1945.

The end of the war forced the USAAF to re-evaluate the Twin Mustang's future and instead of 500 P-82Bs, the Air Force issued a modified procurement order on 7 December 1945 authorizing the construction of 270 P-82Bs, including twenty already under assembly, and 230 P-82E long-range escort fighters. Further production cuts resulted in the delivery of only twenty P-82B aircraft (serial numbers 44-65160 through 65179) with the Air Force taking delivery between November 1945 and March 1946. The entire production block, except for two modified for night fighter evaluation, was assigned to the training of flight crews for the next production variant-the P-82E. The cost for the P-82B was $140,513 per

**Three-quarter profile of the first production P-82B serial number 44-65160. Powered by 1860hp Packard-Merlin engines, its maiden flight occurred 31 October 1945 and was delivered to the Air Force in November of that year.**
*(American Aviation Historical Society)*

P-82B serial number 44-65176 (PQ-176) over Texas *circa* 1947, like her nineteen sisters, P-82Bs were allocated to research and development or training roles. The PQ buzz number stood for 'P' for pursuit and 'Q' for the manufacturer North American Aviation. (*American Aviation Historical Society*)

Assigned to the 325th F(AW)G (Fighter (All-Weather) Group), P-82B serial number 44-65173 (FQ-173), the fourteenth 'B' model, at Hamilton Field, California on 18 September 1948. Note the 'P' for pursuit designator has changed to 'F' for fighter per a then new U.S. Air Force policy. (*Nicholas A. Veronico*)

F-82B serial number 44-65177 (FQ-177) with a F-61 Black Widow assigned to 27th FEG (Fighter Escort Group) and later to the 57th F(AW)G *circa* 1948. This aircraft went on to Shepherd Air Force Base, Texas before being scrapped. (*American Aviation Historical Society*)

unit. The B-model differed from the XP-82 only by the addition of a pressure carburettor on their Packard-Merlin engines along with the actual provision for underwing pylons for ordnance and improved machine guns (the XP-82 was equipped with Mod-2 machine guns while the P-82B received the Mod-3).

A majority of the twenty manufactured P-82Bs were used as training aircraft by the 27th Fighter Escort Group (FEG) based at Kearney Army Air Force Base (AAFB), Nebraska. Two of the -Bs were actually pulled from the production line and

An early production Twin Mustang preparing to land at an undisclosed location. Note the pylons for external ordnance located under each wing and the centre section. (*American Aviation Historical Society*)

The **P-82B** remained in USAF service through December 1949. The last of this type, 44-65179 (FQ-179) shown here, was retained by NACA for testing. (*American Aviation Historical Society*)

F-82B, 44-65179, with Firebrand air-to-air missiles tested at Holloman Air Force Base, New Mexico. The missiles developed by the Ryan Corporation did not go into production. (American Aviation Historical Society)

modified for night interception work. NACA used serial number 44-65179 in missile research while the Air Proving Ground at Eglin Field, Florida, modified and tested 44-65170 as a photographic reconnaissance version called the RF-82. Meanwhile, NAA went on to develop and produce the next Twin Mustang variant, the P-82E, and the Air Force withdrew the -B from service in December 1949.

The P-82B might have faded into oblivion and ended on the scrap heap if not for 44-65168's (the ninth Twin Mustang off the production line) contribution to aviation history by making a non-stop flight on 27-28 February 1947. On that date,

**'Betty Jo' P-82B serial number 44-65168 (PQ-168) being prepared for its non-stop flight from Hawaii to New York during February 1947. This Twin Mustang carried its direction finder in football shaped housings on the fuselage behind each cockpit. The aircraft had red-white-and-blue propeller spinners with red and black lettering for the aircraft's nose art. (Robert F. Dorr)**

'Betty Jo' prepares to depart for Hawaii prior to its record setting Hawaii to New York flight. Commanded by Lieutenant Colonel Robert E. Thacker with co-pilot Lieutenant John M. Ard, the aircraft was christened 'Betty Jo' after Thacker's spouse. A sign painter mistakenly added the masculine 'Joe' to the nose art which was later removed. (*San Diego Aerospace Museum via Nicholas A. Veronico*)

Lieutenant Colonel Robert Thacker and Lieutenant John Ard flew 44-65168, named 'Betty Jo' after Thacker's wife, on a non-stop flight from Hickam Field, Hawaii, to LaGuardia Field on Long Island, New York, in fourteen hours thirty-one minutes and fifty seconds at an average speed of 347mph. They accomplished this feat without refuelling by stripping down the aircraft and adding additional internal fuel tanks and four 310-gallon drop tanks. This aircraft is now restored and displayed at the National Museum of the U.S. Air Force.

For the flight, 'Betty Jo' carried four 310 gallon drop tanks in addition to its internal fuel for a total of 2,215 gallons. Thacker and Ard made the flight in 14 hours, 31 minutes, 50 seconds at an average speed of 347mph. (*Nicholas A. Veronico*)

This map, which appeared in U.S. newspapers at the time, shows the route of the record-breaking flight of 'Betty Jo' during February 1947. (*Nicholas A. Veronico*)

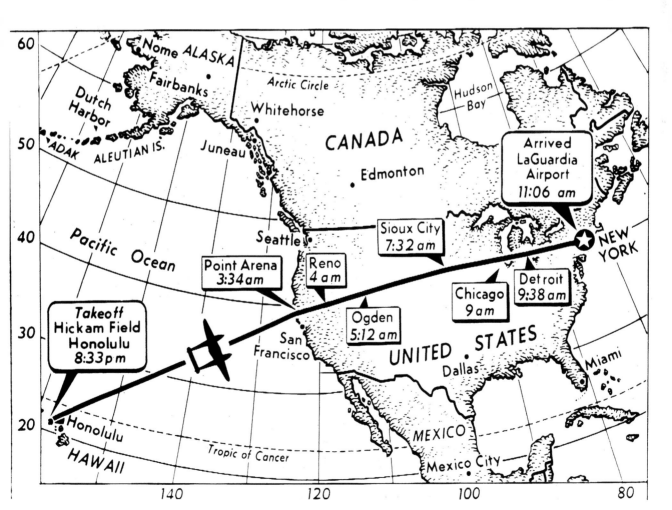

Shortly after the record setting flight, 'Betty Jo,' her name now corrected, returned to Inglewood, California where this photo was taken. After the F-82B was phased out of service, 'Betty Jo' was transferred to NACA. After a successful career in aerospace testing, the aircraft was transferred to the U.S. Air Force Museum. (*San Diego Aerospace Museum via Nicholas A. Veronico*)

# Chapter Two:
# F-82E Long-Range Escort

Air Force interest with the P-82 program continued as there was no alternative long-range escort for the B-50 Superfortress, an improved version of the B-29 with a noticeably higher vertical stabilizer, and the Convair B-36 Peacemaker, then under development, since early jet fighters didn't have the range for long-range escort missions. (The Air Force's front-line jet interceptor, the Lockheed F-80, only had a normal range of approximately 800 miles). Early in the Twin Mustang's development, the government made it no secret that it wanted Allison V-1710 engines to power the P-82 since it had become doubtful that the Packard-Merlin V-1650 would be available much longer. This was largely due to failed negotiations with Rolls-Royce who owned the rights and wanted Packard to pay $6,000 in royalties for every engine that the company produced. Another reason to switch to the Allison was that General Motors (GM), who owned Allison, also owned forty percent of North American Aviation and, with the end of the war, the aircraft industry went into a nose dive and the company needed to sell more Allison engines and parts to keep investors happy.

The P-82E, designated as model NA-144, became the first mass produced model of the Twin Mustang and was powered by the Allison V-1710-143 (right) and 145 (left) engines, which rotated in opposite directions. In February 1946, North American received an order for 250 Allison-powered P-82Es with a finalized contract (AC-13950) for this procurement signed on 10 October 1946. The $35 million procurement contract covered the cost for 250 P-82Es plus tools and spare parts. North American would be paid $17 million for the first 100 planes, $14.5 million for the remaining 150, and $3.5 million for special tools and ground-handling equipment. The Air Force expected the first deliveries to begin in November 1946 and, after the completion of the first 100 aircraft, NAA and the Air Force would review the contract to adjust requirements which it did by ordering the last 150 E models modified as night fighters. NAA test pilot George Welch took the P-82E on its maiden flight on 17 April 1947. The new Twin Mustang model was slightly slower with a top speed of 465mph and a lower rate of climb by almost 900 feet per minute.

Problems with the Allison engines delayed Twin Mustang production for nearly two years as production costs rose to more than $50 million. The government negotiated with Allison in August 1945 to supply North American with an updated V-1710, since earlier versions of the powerplant had equipped the P-38 and P-40, among other famed aircraft from the Second World War. Allison agreed to purchase government parts to develop the new engine, which proved to be costly with a final price tag of $18.5 million. As previously stated the first flight of the P-82E took place on 17 April 1947; however, engine malfunctions appeared during the flight and

**The first production P-82E serial number 46-6255 (PQ-255) was accepted by the U.S. Air Force in September 1947 but was retained by NAA for further flight evaluation. (*Nicholas A. Veronico*)**

144-0-1F

**The first production P-82E parked outside the NAA factory. The first flight of this series occurred on 17 April 1947. The first 100 Allison-powered E models beginning with 46-6255 were officially designated as P-82E-NA. (*Nicholas A. Veronico*)**

continued with the next four aircraft accepted by the Air Force (one each in September and November 1947 and two in December). The updated Allison V-1710 suffered from spark plug fouling, oil leaks, engine backfiring at high and low power settings, auxiliary super-charger failure, and engine power surge. Fouling of the spark plugs caused by oil accumulation was the most serious problem requiring new spark plugs after nearly every single flight.

Because the new engine was not as reliable as the Merlin (it was nicknamed 'The Allison time-bomb'), problems persisted with the engines that required extensive testing through June 1948 using the first four -82E Twin Mustangs. North American had to accept the first 200 Allison engines, which could only operate at lower

The second production P-82E serial number 46-6256 (PQ-256) flying over an undisclosed location during 1947. The most noticeable external differences between the P-82B and E Twin Mustangs was a reconfigured nose to house the P-82E's troublesome 2,250hp Allison V-1710 engines along with twelve exhaust stacks instead of the six found on the P-82B. (U.S. Air Force)

**This bomb-laden F-82E serial number 46-6263 operated with the 27th FEG at Robbins Air Force Base. Although capable of carry 6,000lbs of bombs, the E model Twin Mustang's primary mission was long range bomber escort. (*Robert F. Dorr*)**

power settings, to avoid further F-82 production delays. Meanwhile, as the aircraft company waited for acceptable engines, the cost to North American continued to climb as it had to store uncompleted Twin Mustang airframes in a warehouse owned by the Consolidated-Vultee Aircraft Corporation (Convair) at Downey, California. Assembly lines were set up at Downey to install engines as they arrived and deliver the completed F-82Es rather than truck them back to North American's facility at Inglewood. NAA engineers were able to fix some of the problems by using Merlin components but the engine, along with a shortage of spare parts, continued to be a problem for the F-82 throughout the aircraft's operational life. The F-82Es were externally indistinguishable from the F-82Bs except for a reconfigured nose for the Allison engine with twelve exhaust stacks on each side of the cowling instead of the six that characterized the Packard Merlin.

The P-82E became the F-82E, after the newly established U.S. Air Force changed the pursuit 'P' indicator to 'F' for fighter in 1948. The Air Force accepted 100 F-82Es with serial numbers 46-255 to 46-354, the serial numbers being reduced from 7 digits for the -B series to 5 digits for the E-H series. Actual tail numbering, except for the -B model, consisted of the last number of the relevant fiscal year followed by the three-digit production serial number. Most went to the 27th Fighter Escort Group (FEG) which was comprised of the 522nd, 523rd, and 524th Fighter Interceptor Squadrons (FIS) and were assigned to the newly established Strategic Air Command (SAC) as long-range escorts for B-29, B-50, and B-36 bombers. The F-82E often flew long-range demonstration flights as a propaganda weapon against the Soviets to show the Air Force's ability to protect its strategic bomber force. By the end of fiscal year 1948, North American had delivered seventy-two E-Model

**An Eighth Air Force P-82E serial number 46-6334 parked on an icy tarmac at an unknown location displays the Eighth Air Force emblem below the cockpit. It ended its service life at McClellan Air Force Base, California. (*U.S. Air Force*)**

F-82E serial number 46-6275 (FQ-275) of the 27th FEG's 523rd Fighter Interceptor Squadron (FIS) at Concord, California, on 28 May 1949. This aircraft ended its service life at Robbins Air Force Base. (*Nicholas A. Veronico*)

FQ-275 was the personal aircraft of Colonel Don Blakeslee, future commander of the 27th FEG and 14.5 victory fighter ace during the Second World War. (*William T. Larkins via Nicholas A. Veronico*)

**F-82Es of the 27th FEG returning to Bergstrom Air Force Base, Texas, from Matagorda Island Bombing Range, Texas, during April 1950. The F-82E's original primary mission was to escort very long-range bombers such as the Convair B-36 Peacemaker, which had a range of more than 7,000 miles. (Robert F. Dorr)**

Twin Mustangs with a further twenty-four in fiscal year 1949 at a cost of $215,154 per unit (this was the same cost as applied to the F through H series). The 27th FEG conducted over-water Very Long Range (VLR) training missions beginning in January 1949 which encompassed a five-leg flight starting from Kearney Air Force Base (AFB), Nebraska, to MacDill AFB, Florida, then to Ramey AFB, Puerto Rico, to Howard AFB Panama, then to Jamaica, and then back to Kearney – a trip that took a few days to complete. One VLR mission starting from Bergstrom AFB in Austin, Texas, to Ramey AFB – a distance of some 2,300 miles – was accomplished without refuelling.

An artist-enhanced image showing a flight of F-82Es of the 27th FEG returning to Bergstrom Air Force Base during July 1949. The Group, consisting of 522nd, 523rd, and 524th Fighter Squadrons, served as escort fighters for B-29 bombers. (*Author's Collection*)

The Air Force regarded the F-82E as a short-term interim fighter, and with the promise of jets with longer range plus the arrival of mid-air refuelling with Boeing KC-29 and KC-97 aerial tankers, the Air Force had begun phasing out the F-82E by March 1950, less than a year after the final unit rolled off the assembly line. The 27th FEG started transitioning to the F-84E Thunderjet in the spring of 1950 and by September 1950, the Group's last F-82Es were flown to Warner-Robbins AFB, Georgia. The Air Force made the decision to scrap all of the Twin Mustang escorts, retaining the engines and other usable parts for the remaining F-82F/G/H night and all-weather fighters stationed in Alaska and the Korean War zone.

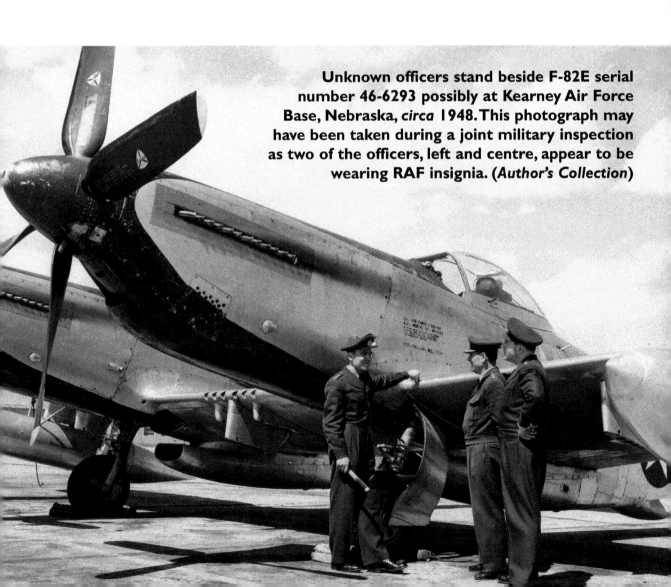

Unknown officers stand beside F-82E serial number 46-6293 possibly at Kearney Air Force Base, Nebraska, *circa* 1948. This photograph may have been taken during a joint military inspection as two of the officers, left and centre, appear to be wearing RAF insignia. (*Author's Collection*)

P, later F-82E, 46-6299 parked between flights at Fairfield-Susuin Air Force Base (now Travis Air Force Base), California. Like many others of its kind, it ended its service life at Robbins Air Force Base. (*William T. Larkins via Nicholas A. Veronico*)

Civilians look into the cockpit of P-82E 46-6339 from the 27th FEG during an airshow possibly at Robbins Air Force Base, Georgia. Beyond is a Black Widow night fighter, an aircraft that would be replaced by the night fighter variant of the Twin Mustang. (*American Aviation Historical Society*)

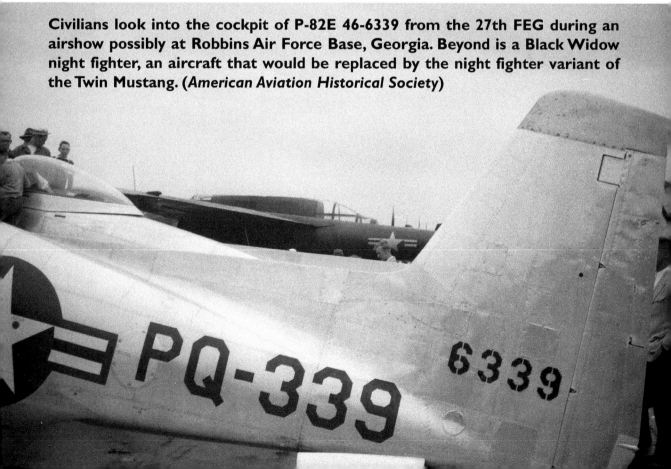

Retained by NAA, PQ-255 has been modified to carry the pressurized radar 'pickle' fitted to later night fighter variants. This aircraft ended its service life with the 27th FEG at Robbins Air Force Base. (Robert F. Dorr)

# Chapter Three:
# Night and
# All-Weather Fighter

The Air Force's first aircraft specifically designed as a night fighter was the twin-engine P-61 Black Widow equipped with the SCR-720 airborne radar. Two prototypes were ordered in January 1941 but, due to technical issues, a prototype did not take to the air until May 1942. Labour and material shortages delayed delivery of the first production P-61A until October 1943 followed by the P-61B in July 1944 and a C-variant in July 1945. The twin-boom Black Widow, armed with 20mm cannons and .50-caliber machine guns, proved far superior to the P-70 – a stop-gap night-fighter adaptation of the Douglas A-20 Havoc/Boston light bomber. Powered by two 2,000-hp Pratt & Whitney engines with two-speed General Electric superchargers, the P-61 had a top speed of 367mph with a rate of climb of 1,775 feet-per-minute. Unfortunately it proved to be a poor interceptor against Japanese bombers above 20,000 feet and the Black Widow's radar operated satisfactory only eighty-one percent of the time, making that system responsible for more abortive missions than any other malfunction. The SCR-720 had a forward search azimuth of 180-degrees with a maximum search range of five to seven miles. However, the Black Widow was the best the Air Force could hope for during that period and it would rely on the P-61 after the war until 1948 when the F-82F and G Twin Mustangs, specially equipped for night fighting duties, became operational.

In November 1945, the Air Force requested an evaluation of the P-82B to see whether it could be adapted to replace the P-61 night fighter. Consequently, North American pulled the tenth and eleventh of the twenty production P-82Bs for conversion into night fighters as the P-82C (serial number 44-65169) and P-82D (serial number 44-65170) in late 1946. The P-82C's maiden flight occurred on 27 March 1947 and the P-82D followed two days later. Both experimental night fighters featured a large radar pod, nicknamed the 'pickle' or 'dong,' under the centre wing section with the C-model housing the SCR-720 radar while the P-82D used the

AN/APS-4 radar. The large nacelle, adopted for the production models F-82F, G, and H, and somewhat resembling a drop tank, protruded forward past the propellers to eliminate interference. A radar operator's position, with related equipment, replaced the co-pilot's instrumentation and controls in the right-hand cockpit.

**Two P-82Bs were modified as night fighter prototypes. In this configuration, the second pilot was replaced by a radar operator. P-82B-1-NA 44-65169 had an SCR-720 radar installed in its centre wing pod becoming the sole P-82C. (*Robert F. Dorr*)**

This is the tenth P-82B produced and was modified as the P-82C night fighter flying over Malibu Beach, California during 1947. Night fighter variants of the Twin Mustang were painted overall glossy black with red codes. (*Nicholas A. Veronico*)

The eleventh production P-82B serial number 46-65170 was pulled from the assembly line and modified as the P-82D. This, the prototype for the F-82F night fighter, was fitted with the AN/APS-4 radar while production F-82Fs were fitted with the AN/APG-28, a modified version of the APS-4. (*U.S. Air Force*)

Frontal view of a night fighter variant showing the bulbous radar nacelle, which didn't reduce the aircraft's performance significantly, but it did reduce the amount of external ordnance that it could carry. *(339th FIS Association via SM/Sgt. Bruce Campbell, USAF)*

An unusual piece of equipment mounted under P-82D, PQ-170, which may be an experimental radar pod. The aircraft can be identified by the barely visible PQ-170 designator applied to the underside of the wing. *(Robert F. Dorr)*

Ramp shot of an unidentified P-82F. As stated earlier this was the production version of the solitary P-82D night fighter albeit with the **APG-28** radar installed in the centre wing pod. F models were built and served with the **U.S. Air Force's Air Defense Command (ADC)**. All F-82Fs were delivered by the end of 1949. *(Nicholas A. Veronico)*

**F-82F, FQ-408, serial number 46-408 of the 52nd F(AW)G sporting a colourful tail-assembly of overall blue with gold stars and stripes. Twin Mustangs of the 52nd F(AW)G (Fighter All-Weather Group) protected the eastern United States during the late 1940s before the group transitioned to the Lockheed F-94B. (*Author's Collection*)**

**FQ-433 of the 52nd F(AW)G, serial number 46-433 at Mitchell Field Air Force Base, New York. This aircraft was assigned to an Element Leader indicated by the single white band around the fuselage behind the cockpit. The tail is medium blue with silver stripes and stars. (*Author's Collection*)**

**Snow-covered ramp shot of an unidentified F-82F belonging to the 325th F(AW)G, possibly at McChord or Moses Lake Air Force Base, Washington State,** *circa* **1949. (***Robert F. Dorr***)**

One hundred examples of the D variant were produced as the P-82F (model NA-149 with serial numbers 46-405 to 46-504) equipped with the AN/APG-28 – an improved version of the APS-4 radar – with an additional forty-five of the C variant as the P-82G (model NA-150 with serial numbers 46-355 to 46-383 and 46-389 to 46-404 equipped with the SCR 720). The additional weight of the radar pod created very few performance problems with the F-82F having a top speed of

F-82F serial number 46-461 at McChord Air Force Base during early 1952 where the Twin Mustang-equipped 325th F(AW)G flew air defence as the only all-weather fighter group for the north-western United States. (*Robert F. Dorr*)

Another F-82F belonging to the 325th F(AW)G was 46-420 which operated from McChord Air Force Base. It was later cannibalized (during mid-to-late 1951) to provide spare parts for other Twin Mustangs. (*Author's Collection*)

The radar cockpit of F, G and H models contained no flight or power plant controls. The right-hand cockpit, intended for use by a radar operator, only contained controls and instruments necessary for the operation of the radar equipment. The SCR radar indicator is in the centre. (*Gerald Balzer Collection via Richard Dann*)

460mph. The G's SCR-720 radar weighed slightly less than the APG-28 and thus the aircraft's performance was slightly better. Before NAA delivered either the F or the G, the Air Force requested an additional requirement for modifying a small number of the night variants into all-weather fighters for service in Alaska; nine F-82Fs (serial numbers 46-496 through 46-504) and five additional F-82Gs (serial numbers 46-384 through 46-388). The F-82H was the last Twin Mustang variant produced and

**Control of the Twin Mustang F, G, and H models lay solely with the pilot in the left cockpit, while the radar operator's cockpit was on the right. Shown here is the pilot's cockpit of the G and H Models. (*Gerald Balzer Collection via Richard Dann*)**

A pair of F-82Fs of the 325th F(AW)G depart Hamilton Field, California, for an air defence sortie on 18 September 1948. The group relocated from Mitchell Field to Hamilton in April 1947. (*Nicholas A. Veronico*)

Three F-82s at Hamilton Field (later Air Force Base), California, with the engine cowlings removed from one of them undergoing maintenance. FQ-437 in the foreground was an F-82F. (*Author's Collection*)

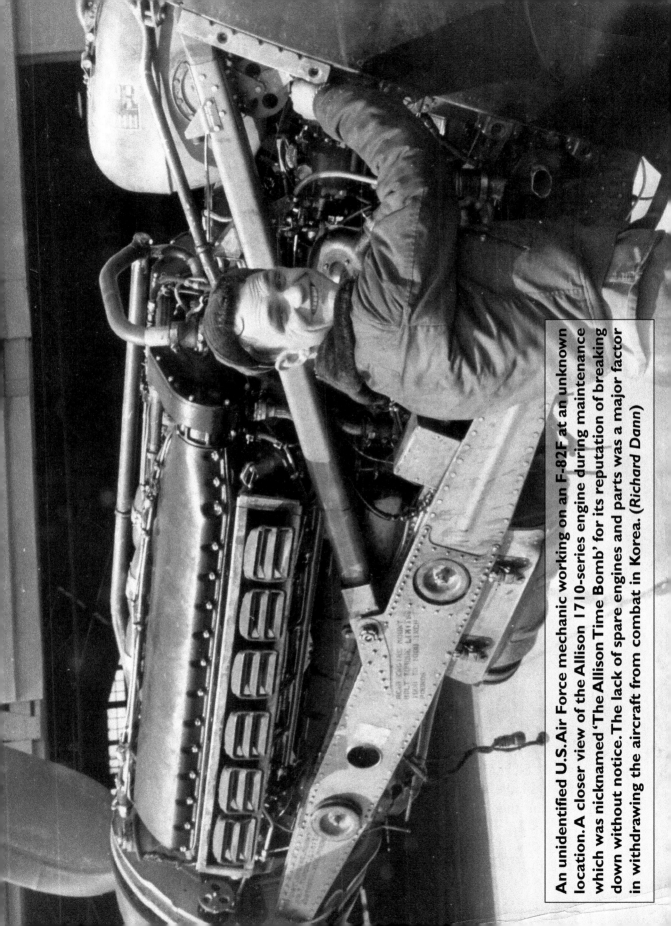

An unidentified U.S. Air Force mechanic working on an F-82F at an unknown location. A closer view of the Allison 1710-series engine during maintenance which was nicknamed 'The Allison Time Bomb' for its reputation of breaking down without notice. The lack of spare engines and parts was a major factor in withdrawing the aircraft from combat in Korea. (*Richard Dann*)

**F-82F serial number 46-415 which was the eleventh F-82F produced. 46-415 was one of the few F variants to operate in the Korean Theatre of operations during the conflict serving with the 68th F(AW)S. (*Howard Levy via Robert F. Dorr*)**

was specially equipped with thermal anti-icing gear and de-icer boots on the propeller blades. The thermal de-icing equipment sent hot air from behind the after-cooler radiator and blew it across the wing leading edges and tail surfaces. Other modifications included an improved cockpit heating system, updated radio equipment, plus the SCR-720 radar with which the F-82G was already equipped.

The F, G, and H Twin Mustang was not a pilot's ideal night fighter due to the cockpit's limited field of view, and poor landing characteristics especially at night. Moreover, during nocturnal operations, the pilot and radar operator found it difficult to maintain night vision due to engine exhaust flame, instrument glare and the bright flashes from the aircraft's machine guns. The Air Force accepted the last F-82G and six F-82H Twin Mustangs in March 1949.

By mid-1950, the Twin Mustang had become a second-line aircraft as squadrons began replacing them with the jet-powered F-89 and F-94. From an operational

FQ-426 engine run-up at Hamilton Field Air Force Base on 18 September 1948 while operating with the 325th F(AW)G. It went on to Lowry Air Force Base, Colorado, where it was written off in an operational accident during October 1949. (Nicholas A. Veronico)

**F-82F, FQ-470, serial number 46-470 with rocket rails mounted under the wing belonged to the 325th F(AW)G. According to records it was stricken from the U.S. Air Force inventory in May 1948 at Brooks Air Force Base, Texas. (*Nicholas A. Veronico*)**

standpoint, some pilots felt a psychological discomfort of impending doom of a mid-air collision when they caught sight of the co-pilot/radar operator's fuselage out of the corner of their eyes. Another problem was with the J-8 Altitude Gyro used during instrument flying. Pilots either loved it or hated it because it read exactly opposite to the presentation of conventional gyroscopic instruments. When the miniature aircraft on the gyro appeared 'below' the reference line, instead of descending the F-82 was actually climbing and so, during an instrument landing approach, the pilot had to remain cognizant of what the aircraft was actually doing.

The F-82F first flew on 11 March 1948 and entered service in September with the Air Defense Command to replace the P-61 Black Widow, while the F-82G had become operational by the end of 1948 with the Caribbean Air Command: the Fifth, and Twentieth Air Force for the Far East Air Forces (FEAF). The Air Force established two all-weather fighter groups – the 52nd Fighter (All-Weather) Group (F(AW)G) and 325th F(AW)G – with the first F-82Fs going to the 52nd F(AW)G. These F-82 night fighter air groups provided air defence of the CONUS (Continental United States) from early 1948 to mid-1952 when conversion to the Lockheed F-94A/B was completed. The first F-82H flew on 15 February 1949 and all fourteen went to the 449th Fighter (All-Weather) Squadron (F(AW)S) based at Ladd AFB, with detachments operating from Galena, Davis, and Mark Fields, Alaska. The last F-82H remained on the USAF inventory until June 1953. The 449th flew periodic armed-reconnaissance missions over the coastline of western Russia (Chukchi Peninsula), between May 1949 and July 1950, along with challenging Soviet reconnaissance aircraft that neared Alaskan airspace. An unusual series of missions flown by the 449th during May 1949 was bombing ice jams in Alaskan rivers to prevent flooding.

Problems with the lacklustre performance of the Allison V-1710 engine caused nearly a two-year delay in the production and delivery of the F-82E, and by that time the Air Force had reduced the procurement order to 250 E through H variants. The F-82 was the last piston-engined fighter accepted by the Air Force in large numbers; it was an interim fighter, a stop-gap measure needed to fill a void until the arrival of modern jet fighters with greater range and night fighting capabilities. The Twin Mustang would have faded into oblivion except for the record-breaking flight of the

**FQ-434 at Hamilton Air Force Base on 18 September 1948 as part of the 325th F(AW)G. This aircraft, like many of her sisters, became a source of spare parts when it was flown to Hill Air Force Base, Utah, in 1949. (*Nicholas A. Veronico*)**

An unidentified F-82F carrying air sampling pods under its wings sits on the ramp at Wright-Patterson Air Force Base in the late 1940s. The air sampling pods were used for weather research. (*U.S. Air Force*)

From front to rear are all-weather F-82H Twin Mustangs FQ-384, 497, and 386 belonging to the 449th F(AW)S based at Ladd Air Force Base, Alaska. FQ-384 was originally a G model from the 4th F(AW)S with the nose art name of 'Wee Pea II'. (*Robert F. Dorr via Glenn L. Jackson*)

**The photographs on this and the previous page show how the F-82's nose design and engine exhaust stacks evolved over time. The first image shows the nose and engine exhausts of a B model, followed by the F-82E – which sported a deeper chin and twelve exhaust stubs per side. Finally, the F-82F, G and H night and all-weather variants were fitted with flame dampening exhausts. (NASA, American Aviation Historical Society, and Nicholas A. Veronico)**

F-82B 'Betty Jo,' delays in the production of the Northrop F-89 and Lockheed F-94 all-weather jets, and the unforeseen Korean War. F-82-equipped USAF squadrons saw intense service in the Korean War flying escort, weather reconnaissance, night combat air patrol (NCAP), and interdiction missions between June 1950 and February 1952 before being phased out and replaced by the F-94B. The principal variant of the Twin Mustang to operate in Korea was the F-82G night fighter which, in the new age of jet interceptors, scored the recently established Air Force's first aerial kills only two days after the war began. Ultimately, the lack of spare parts, maintenance issues, and the arrival of jet all-weather fighters ended the F-82's combat duty over Korea.

The last operational F-82 Twin Mustang in active service, FQ-377, serial number 46-377, was used as target tug by the 449th F(AW)S at Ladd Air Force Base. It was an ex-Korean War aircraft formerly operated by the 339th and 4th F(AW)S. (*U.S. Air Force*)

The same aircraft as previously, F-82G, FQ-377, is seen at Ladd AFB, Alaska, during 1952 with drop tanks but lacking its radar pod and the customary black colouration seen on the F and G model night fighter variants having been repainted with high-gloss red on the tail surfaces and outer wing panels. (U.S. Air Force)

# Chapter Four:
# Twins over Korea

On the Sunday of 24 June 1950 at 04.00 hours (25 June Korean Time), seven infantry divisions of the North Korean People's Army (NKPA), supported by one armoured division, equipped with Russian-built T-34 tanks, crossed the 38th parallel into the Republic of South Korea (ROK). Within four days, NKPA forces captured Seoul and continued southward down the peninsula, sweeping aside ROK forces, which fell back southward to Suwon. The United States initially committed air and ground forces to provide military assistance to South Korean Forces and for the protection of women and children dependents of American military personnel and civilians. On the 26th, President Truman committed U.S. forces to enforce the UN Security Council's demand that member states provide military assistance to the Republic Of Korea and named General Douglas MacArthur as Commander-in-Chief, Far East (CINCFE) of all United Nation forces. The air component of Far East Command (FEC) responsible for providing defensive air cover, was the Far East Air Force (FEAF) under the command of Lieutenant General George E. Stratemeyer with the Fifth Air Force based in Japan as its largest component commanded by Major General Earle E. Partridge. American naval and air forces quickly went into action with the Seventh U.S. Fleet establishing a blockade of the Korean Coast while FEAF struck North Korean targets affecting the safety of evacuating American nationals. On 27 June FEAF specifically instructed the Fifth Air Force to establish air superiority over South Korea and strike NKPA ground forces by conducting air strikes against enemy troop concentrations and supply routes.

The arrival of the Twin Mustang over Korea was in response to the evacuation of U.S. civilians, including many women and children, from the advancing North Korean Army to ships in Inchon Harbor or by transport aircraft at nearby Kimpo and Suwon Airfields. Fearing that the North Korean Air Force might try to shoot down the transport aircraft or attack shipping in the harbour, the Air Force requested fighter cover while the ships and transports loaded and departed. Colonel John 'Jack' Price, commander of the Eighth Air Wing immediately realized the difficulties in undertaking this mission since this task required continuous air cover by long-range conventional aircraft. The F-80 Shooting Star was available, but without secure airfields in Korea from which to operate, its thirsty jet engines and an 800-mile combat range (less when fitted with external weapons stores), meant

**Four F-82Gs of the 4th F(AW)S photographed from a fifth Twin Mustang display a variety of nose art. Each aircraft carries the Squadron's insignia of Fu-Jin, the Japanese typhoon god, on their vertical stabilizers. A curious point is the number one and number three aircraft have no radar operators aboard. (*Nicholas A. Veronico*)**

An F-82G from the 4th F(AW)S possibly at Okinawa prior to the unit's transfer to the 347th Fighter All-Weather Group and subsequent combat over Korea. The 347th consisted of the 4th, 68th, and 339th Fighter All-Weather Squadrons and was the sole operator of the F-82G in the Far East. The 4th Squadron conducted only 44 missions over Korea before being recalled to Naha, Okinawa on 8 July 1950. (Robert F. Dorr)

U.S. Air Force armourers make last minute adjustments to the gun bay of an unknown 347th F(AW)G Twin Mustang that is preparing to depart for a mission over Korea. (Author's Collection)

**Four F-82Gs belonging to the 347th F(AW)G, probably from the 68th F(AW)S, above an unknown airfield *circa* 1950. Twin Mustangs appeared over South Korea on 26-27 June 1950 with the primary mission of protecting evacuees fleeing from advancing North Korean Forces. (*Author's Collection*)**

it could only remain over the airfield for a few minutes before having to return to base. The F-82G was the only interceptor capable of travelling the 300-plus miles from Itazuke to the Seoul/Han River area and still have enough fuel to orbit for any length of time and then return to base. He needed the services of three Air Force F-82 squadrons stationed on mainland Japan and Okinawa.

Price had at his disposal twelve F-82Gs of the 68th F(AW)S 'Lightning Lancers' at Itazuke Air Base Kyushu, Japan but that was not nearly enough for the mission. The Fifth Air Force requested the use of Royal Australian Air Force (RAAF) F-51 Mustangs but Britain and the Commonwealth had not yet committed their military

Officers and enlisted personnel of the 68th F(AW)S pose for a unit photograph *circa* 1950. The Squadron was attached to the 8th Fighter-Bomber Wing at Itazuke, Japan before being transferred to the 347th F(AW)G. (Robert F. Dorr)

to the conflict. Therefore, the Fifth Air Force ordered the 339th F(AW)S to move its Twin Mustangs from Yokota, Japan, to join the 68th at Itazuke. The deployment of those two squadrons was still not enough and Brigadier General Jarred V. Crabb, FEAF Director of Operations, ordered the Twentieth Air Force to send eight F-82s from the 4th F(AW)S to Itazuke from their base Naha Air Base, Okinawa. The Air Force quickly formed the three night fighter squadrons into the 347th Fighter (All-Weather) Group (F(AW)G) under the command of Lieutenant Colonel John F. Sharp, commanding officer of the 4th F(AW)S, nicknamed the 'Fightin' Fuujins,' after the Okinawan god of wind. The 347th had an official strength of thirty-three F-82s in late June 1950 but in reality the number ready for combat stood at nineteen: the 4th F(AW)S having five of eleven aircraft combat ready, the 68th with six of ten, and the 339th with eight of twelve. The Air Force, without a long-range jet night fighter, pressed the F-82 into conducting every type of air warfare in Korea from air-to-air combat, bombing, close-air support, weather reconnaissance, air control of ground fire, to night intruder missions. It was one of the 68th F(AW)S Twin Mustang's, piloted by First Lieutenant George D. Deans with radar operator Second Lieutenant Marvin R. Olsen which, during a reconnaissance flight over South Korea on the night of 24/25 June, confirmed the North Korean military had crossed the 38th Parallel.

**Three F-82G Twin Mustangs of the 339th F(AW)S line up at Itazuke Air Base, Japan possibly during summer 1950. Each of the aircraft sport personal art with FQ-379 'The Dull Tool' followed by FQ-395 'The Beast of the Far East,' and FQ-356 'Lackin Blackin.' (*Author's Collection*)**

# Air-to-Air Combat

Aerial coverage by Twin Mustangs began on the morning of 26 June with flights of four F-82s orbiting the Seoul/Inchon area throughout the day as cover for evacuees heading towards the port of Inchon. The first few hours of that first day went by without any trouble but at 13.33 hours a pair of North Korean Lavochin La-7, (Russian-built) fighters appeared and bounced two of the 68th Squadron's Twin Mustangs. One of the F-82s, piloted by Lieutenant William A. 'Skeeter' Hudson with his radar operator Lieutenant Carl S. Fraser, was in the process of providing cover for two ships in Inchon Harbor when the pair of North Korean fighters attacked. Hudson and Fraser were under the assumption that the existing rules of engagement restricted any offensive action and they could only defend themselves if fired upon by hostile forces. According to Fraser, 'We were supposed to be fighter cover for the two evacuation boats at Inchon, but after we were there for about thirty minutes, our control radioed us to proceed inland to Kimpo Air Base and cover the motor convoy bringing people from Seoul to Inchon,' he said.

'Skeeter' Hudson's aircraft with another Twin Mustang went inland at an altitude of 500 feet while two other F-82s provided top cover above the clouds at 3,000 feet. 'After going up and down the road a couple of times, we spotted a couple of Russian-made Lavochkin LA-7s, at 11 o'clock high. We were instructed not to fire unless fired upon, so we didn't make any aggressive move in their direction,' Fraser said. 'They started a wide turn toward us and we started one to keep them in sight. Suddenly, the leader tightened up his turn and peeled off at us, with the wingman right behind him. When we saw that he was going to attack, we dropped our external tanks, put on the combat power, turned on the gun switches and started a climbing turn toward him.' The F-82s were under the impression not to engage until fired upon. Fraser continued, 'Since we were forced to wait for him to make the aggressive move, he was in a good position to clobber us, but he was either overeager, or green, because he started firing from too far out and his bullets lagged behind us for the entire firing pass. His wingman started to make his pass on our wingman, but he wasn't in a good enough position to even fire. They broke off and started a turn around on our tails, so we pulled up through the overcast. We figured that, if they came up through, we'd be up there in a position to let them have it. They evidently decided not to press the matter, because they never showed up.'

The Twin Mustang pilots' decision not to engage the enemy infuriated Far East Command and it sent an order to FEAF that mandated its fighters to engage and destroy any NKPA aircraft approaching Republic of Korea and American forces. On the 27th, FEAF clarified the rules of engagement in which U.S. fighters would engage any North Korean military aircraft operating over South Korea; this clarification led to the 68th and 339th scoring the first aerial kills by USAF fighters. Evacuations in the Inchon area continued but Colonel Price became concerned over the effectiveness of F-82 squadrons due to aircrew fatigue – one pilot had flown fifteen hours out of the last thirty-eight but Price had no other choice: the Twin Mustangs had to continue with the mission because of their long-range capability. Operations on 27 June 1950 became the F-82's high watermark as a (night) fighter in combat. Eleven Twin Mustangs belonging to the 4th, 68th, and 339th F(AW)S squadrons in conjunction with F-80C Shooting Stars of the 8th Fighter-Bomber Wing (FBW) took turns providing cover for the Norwegian freighter *Reinholte* evacuating civilians

**Enlisted U.S. Air Force maintenance personnel taking a break while Japanese labourers in the background appear to be looking towards F-82G Twin Mustang FQ-404 operated first by the 339th and then the 68th F(AW)S. It was later transferred to the 449th F(AW)S at Elmendorf Air Force Base, Alaska, and became a source of spare parts. (*Author's Collection*)**

A pair of F-82Gs at a maintenance area for the 339th F(AW)S in Japan *circa* 1950 with FQ-356 in the foreground. The aircraft's drop tank in the background has a white number seven applied to it which corresponded to the in-squadron codex found on the tails of the Squadron's aircraft. *(339th FIS Association via SMSgt. Bruce Campbell, USAF)*

at Inchon Harbor and for a similar mission of a Douglas C-54 transport aircraft at Kimpo Air Base. Four F-82s of the 68th orbited an area around Kimpo Airfield and Suwon at 4,000 feet while three 339th Twin Mustangs flew at 8,000 feet and four more fighters of the 4th F(AW)S provided top cover at 12,000 feet. Flying above the evacuation Carl Fraser and 'Skeeter' Hudson were not about to repeat the previous day's event and the team would engage in the first air-to-air engagement and record FEAF's first aerial kill of the conflict.

The formation flew above the evacuation playing out below in Inchon Harbor and Kimpo for nearly three hours until five enemy aircraft; Ilyushin Il-10 *Sturmovik* and Yakovlev Yak-7s (some sources cite Lavochkin La-7s or La-9s as participants) jumped the American fighters at 11.50 hours. Dropping out of the clouds, one of the North Korean fighters selected the last F-82 in the 68th Squadron's formation, FQ-357, piloted by Lieutenant Charles 'Chalky' Moran with Lieutenant Fred Larkins

**A side profile of the 68th F(AW)S FQ-383 displaying natural aluminium drop tanks with the vertical tail displaying the Squadron's emblem of a medieval knight. Lieutenant William 'Skeeter' Hudson and radar operator Lieutenant Carl Fraser operated this aircraft and scored the first official aerial kill of the Korean War. (*U.S. Air Force*)**

as the radar operator and began firing, scoring several hits on the Twin Mustang's vertical stabilizer, but Moran's faster and more agile night fighter successfully eluded the attacker and his aircraft suffered no further damage. According to Carl Fraser, 'It was while we were circling Kimpo that two North Korean fighters came up out of some low clouds and started after Charlie Moran, who was the number-four man in our flight. Their shooting was a little better this time, and they shot up Charlie's tail.' The F-82 pilots broke away as the enemy fighters flashed by the formation but the slower North Korean aircraft proved no match for the faster Twin Mustangs as they accelerated and manoeuvred behind their adversaries. 'Skeeter' Hudson conducted a high-G turn and latched onto one of the enemy aircraft. 'Hudson slipped around and got on one of their tails,' Fraser said. 'When the guy realized that we were there, he pulled up into some clouds, and tried to shake us.' Fraser continued, 'We were so close to him that we could even see him in the middle of the clouds.'

Following the North Korean aircraft through the clouds and down to an altitude of 1,000 feet or less, Lieutenant Hudson lined up his Mk-18 gun sight and blasted away with the F-82's six .50-caliber machine guns scoring hits on the enemy plane and knocking off pieces of the fuselage. The Yak banked steeply to the right as a second burst from Hudson's fighter tore off the flap and aileron, ignited the gas tank, and caught the right wing afire. 'By this time we were in so close we almost collided with him,' Fraser said. Hudson and Fraser then observed the enemy pilot climb out of his cockpit of the stricken plane and onto the wing, turning around and speaking to the observer still strapped inside the rear cockpit. The observer, petrified, dead, or wounded, did not move as the North Korean pilot pulled his parachute's ripcord. The chute billowed which yanked the man off the aircraft. At that moment, Fraser grabbed his 35mm camera he had taken aloft and snapped a photo. The enemy plane then rolled over with the observer still inside and crashed into the ground. The North Korean pilot survived his escape from the burning plane and landed safely but he was shot to death by South Korean troops after he started shooting at them with a pistol.

A few minutes later, Lieutenant Moran managed to latch onto the tail of the Yak that had made the initial attack on him and shot the plane down over Kimpo. At the beginning of the engagement, when the North Korean fighter had shot up his aircraft's tail, Moran pulled the stick hard back but his aircraft began to stall and

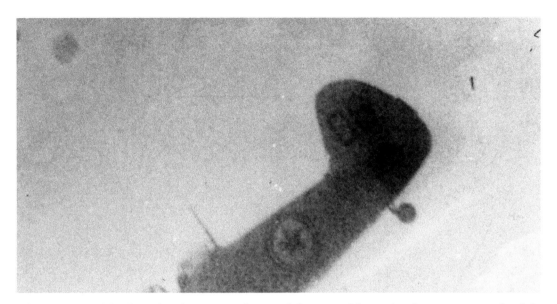

**Lieutenant Hudson's victory taken with a malfunctioning camera by his radar operator, Lieutenant Fraser. The North Korean insignia and the observer in the rear cockpit are just visible. The observer failed to parachute and went down with the aircraft. The pilot bailed out and landed by South Korean troops who shot and killed him after he fired at them with a handgun. (*U.S Air Force*)**

started to drop making it an easy target for the enemy. Moran jammed his stick forward to recover and as his aircraft responded the Yak appeared right in front of him and a few bursts from the F-82's guns sent the North Korean crashing to the ground. Sadly, Lieutenant Moran, along with his radar operator Lieutenant Francis J. Meyer, were killed in action less than two months later on 7 August 1950 when their Twin Mustang crashed into a hill after hitting a cable that the North Koreans had strung across a valley. The wreckage of his aircraft, serial 46-355, and the crew's remains were found 18 months later by ROK forces.

The three Twin Mustangs of the 339th Squadron, flying mid cover for the formation, joined in the fray with Lieutenant Walt Hayhurst and radar operator Lieutenant Cliff Miles latching onto another enemy fighter from the rear and opening fire at almost point-blank range of 100 yards scoring hits along the length

Lieutenant Charles 'Chalky' Moran and radar operator Lieutenant Fred Larkins with the 68th F(AW)S flew F-82G, FQ-357 and scored one confirmed kill shooting down a North Korean fighter. (*Robert F. Dorr*)

Lieutenant Moran's F-82 received some damage to the tail area caused by an enemy aircraft's machine gun fire during the 27 June battle. Moran would be killed in action two months later flying another F-82G serial number 46-355. (*U.S. Air Force*)

of the fuselage. Hayhurst and Miles would have completed dispatching the North Korean except the F-82 was forced to break away to avoid a collision. Immediately, Captain David Texler and Lieutenant Victor Helfenbein, another 339th team, closed in with the same aircraft but lost it in the clouds. Meanwhile, Major James A. 'Poke' Little, commanding officer of the 339th, scored the third and final victory of the day for the Twin Mustangs by taking on the wingman of the aircraft that Hayhurst and Texler had engaged. Chasing the Yak through the clouds, he dispatched the enemy fighter a couple of miles outside Kimpo. The remaining two North Korean fighters seeing three of their brethren fall to the F-82Gs fled the scene. The three aerial victories by the 68th and 339th F(AW)S on 27 June 1950 were the first and last recorded by the Twin Mustang, although, subsequently, another 14 enemy aircraft were destroyed on the ground by F-82s. Later that day, three F-80Cs shot down

Lieutenant Walter Hayhurst of the 339th F(AW)S sits in the pilot's cockpit as his aircraft flies along with FQ-356, 'Lackin Blackin.' Hayhurst participated in the first and only aerial engagement of the Korean War between Twin Mustangs and enemy aircraft. Note weathering on the canopy frame and cockpit's internal antennae along the top of canopy. *(339th FIS Association via SMSgt. Bruce Campbell, USAF)*

**Lieutenant Walter Hayhurst of the 339th F(AW)S in an undated photograph is greeted after completing a mission. He and his radar operator Lieutenant Cliff Miles were credited with the probable destruction of two North Korean aircraft during the 27 June 1950 aerial battle. (*339th FIS Association via SM/Sgt. Bruce Campbell, USAF*)**

four North Korean fighters attacking Kimpo airfield becoming the first jet aircraft victories of the war, despite which however, enemy aircraft did manage to strafe and bomb Suwon airfield, 19 miles south of Kimpo, where they destroyed an F-82 named 'B.O. Plenty' (which had been forced to land at the airfield due to battle damage), as well as a Douglas C-54.

The fast pace in which the North Korean aircraft were engaged, and as to which

**Lieutenant Charles 'Chalky' Moran on the left, in the centre a sergeant writes out an intelligence report on the aerial battle of 27 June 1950. Second from right is Lieutenant William Hudson while crouching is Lieutenant Carl Fraser, the radar operator who flew with Hudson. (*U.S. Air Force*)**

Lieutenant William 'Skeeter' Hudson's crew chief climbing into the cockpit of F-82G, FQ-383, sometime after the 27 June 1950 aerial engagement with North Korean aircraft. Below and to the right of the crew chief is a small red star representing the first air-to-air kill of the Korean War. (Author's Collection)

of them was shot down first, created some confusion regarding which F-82 crew actually scored the first victory and who was piloting which 68th Squadron aircraft at the time. Major Little's and Lieutenant Hudson's victories occurred at approximately the same time. Officially, in 1953, the Fifth Air Force, after reviewing conflicting testimony, credited Lieutenant Hudson with the first kill. The action took place in a matter of a few minutes, therefore, the Air Force's conclusion reached in 1953 must stand unless additional documentation comes to light that may reverse the official record.

# Chapter Five:
# Interdiction and Air Support Missions

By 1 July 1950, American F-80 fighters had effectively stopped incursions by North Korean aircraft below the 38th Parallel and thus eliminated any chance of Twin Mustangs to engage in air-to-air combat. A limited number of F-82s, primarily those of the 68th F(AW)S 'Lightning Lancers,' provided close air support, night interdiction, and night combat air patrol for the remainder of 1950 through early 1951. Until the arrival of carrier and ground-based U.S. Navy and Marine Corps assigned Vought Corsair F4U-5N and Grumman F7F-3N Tigercat night-fighter units, FEAF had to rely on the F-82 to provide combat air patrol and, when required, close air support and interdiction strikes. The Fifth Air Force pressed the small number of Twin Mustangs to fill that void until such replacements arrived. The F-82s standard combat ordnance typically consisted of the inner bomb racks carrying five-inch HVAR rockets mounted on 'trees,' with provision for adding additional 'trees' on the outer bomb racks. The aircraft could carry 2,000lbs of bombs or two 165-gallon napalm tanks in place of the external fuel tanks. F-82G crews noted two problems when carrying external loads. First, the wing tanks had a tendency to whip back and hit the ailerons instead of falling cleanly away. Secondly,  their pilots soon realized that the HVAR rockets had to be fired individually during night missions instead of in salvos since the glare from rapid firing ruined crews' night vision. Additionally, the aircraft in all three of the 347th Group's squadrons developed problems with their pressurized radar pod which, at various times, meant that the group could only depend on operating a third of its F-82Gs as night fighters. Several F-82s either lost or sustained serious damage to the pods as a result of conducting low-level ground support or interdiction missions. The radar's magnetron, housed in a nitrogen-pressurized pod, became useless when a leak occurred thus restricting the now radar-less aircraft to day work.

A day after making the historical first aerial victories of the Korean War on 27

Flight crews of the 68th F(AW)S considered FQ-383 a 'lucky aircraft' as it sustained a considerable amount of battle damage while engaged in close air support and interdiction strikes but, it managed to bring her various crews safely home each time. Putty was often used to fill in damage along the leading edges of the wings. (*Richard Dann*)

June 1950, F-82 squadrons, along with B-26 Invaders and F-80s, flew interdiction missions against North Korean armour, artillery positions, troop columns, supply depots, ground transportation and bridges between the 38th Parallel and friendly positions. On one close air support strike on 29 June, the 68th provided most of the close air support for friendly ground forces dropping napalm-converted fuel tanks on NKPA positions. War is a 24-hour-a-day business requiring the ability to attack an enemy under any conditions, especially at night or during adverse weather and, less than a week after hostilities began, the night air group lost a Twin Mustang and crew as result of poor visibility and possibly a malfunctioning gyroscope. After providing CAP for the Norwegian ship *Reinholte* and striking enemy ground targets four F-82s, returning to Itazuke Air Base, found visibility was down to nearly zero. Ground Control Approach guided three of the aircraft down to safe landings but FQ-358, flown by First Lieutenant Darrell Sayer of the 339th, crashed into a hillside killing both Sayer and his radar operator First Lieutenant Vernon A. Lindvig.

By 1 July 1950, NKPA forces captured Seoul and continued their advance southward until American and ROK ground forces were forced to defend an area around the South Korean port of Pusan at the tip of the Peninsula. U.S. fighters and bombers attempted to slow the advance by pounding enemy forces so hard that most daytime movements were halted. Colonel John F. Sharp approached General Edward J. Timberlake, FEAF combat operations commander, on 2 July requesting

A member of the ground crew poses next to FQ-356 while others steam clean the aircraft. All three of the 347th F(AW)G operated this particular aircraft beginning with the 68th F(AW)S before being written off in an operational accident at Naha Air Base, Okinawa in August 1950. (*Author's Collection*)

that his F-82s be allowed to conduct night interdiction strikes since the enemy had switched to moving primarily during the hours of darkness. The General reluctantly agreed but only with the provision that such a strike be conducted by a single Twin Mustang since it was the only night fighter available in the Far East at the time as well as the only aircraft with the capability of flying over 300 miles from Itazuke to the area around Seoul and stay on station for a significant amount of time. Colonel Sharp took off that evening, at midnight, with his radar operator Captain Cecil Wills guiding the aircraft through the darkness and heavy overcast through his radar mapping skills. The Twin Mustang flew above the Han River towards Seoul at 200 feet; ahead of them stood a bridge with heavy truck traffic heading south. The pilot armed his guns and fired setting trucks afire, continuing down the river's northern bank at an altitude of 50 feet, Sharp fired again at a concentration of military supplies stacked in the open and in the back of trucks. The attack took only a few seconds but it proved the viability of conducting night intruder and interdiction missions with radar-equipped combat aircraft. Such night interdiction missions were

**A 68th F(AW)S F-82G on strip alert at Itazuke Air Base in August 1950 armed with five HVAR rockets beneath the port wing. During the first hectic months of the war Twin Mustangs were pressed into interdiction strikes against North Korea forces as they advanced down the peninsular. (U.S. Air Force)**

F-82G 'The Dull Tool' belonging to the 339th F(AW)S operated from Johnson and Misawa Air Base, Japan, during the Korean War with the Squadron seeing action over Korea during the first weeks of the war. The two individuals in the aircraft are identified as Captain Williams and Lieutenant Helfenbein. *(339th FIS Association via SM/Sgt. Bruce Campbell, USAF)*

extremely hazardous requiring the radar operator to adjust his radar to ground mapping and for the pilot to have the utmost confidence in his radar operator's ability as their aircraft skirted mountains, hills, and weaved through valleys in the darkness. The danger increased when the enemy began stringing steel cable across the valleys with the intent to bring down unsuspecting American night fighters.

Whether it was enemy fire, a steel cable, or a navigational error the air group lost an F-82 and crew on 6 July 1950 when Captain Ernest C. 'Fieb' Fiebelkorn and First Lieutenant John J. Higgins were killed in action near Chongmong-ni, South Korea, during an interdiction mission. Fiebelkorn was a Second World War combat veteran who had served in the European Theatre of Operations scoring nine aerial victories against the Luftwaffe while assigned to the 20th Fighter Group. He stayed in the military after the war serving in the newly formed USAF Reserve before being recalled to active duty with the 4th F(AW)S on Okinawa prior to the Korean conflict. The mission on the sixth involved four Twin Mustangs sent to locate and destroy enemy forces advancing south but after several hours trying to see through the dense overcast Fiebelkorn in F-82G, serial number 46-402, reported to the others he would descend in attempt to find a break in the cloud cover; that was his last communication. Two years later the wreckage along with the remains of Captain Fiebelkorn and his radar observer Captain John L. Higgins were discovered on a mountainside. As mentioned earlier, a similar fate befell Lieutenant 'Chalky' Moran and his radar operator Lieutenant Francis J. Mayer a month later on 7 August.

The existence of the 347th F(AW)G disappeared just as fast as it was created, lasting only ten days from inception on 25 June to its disestablishment on 6 July. The

FEAF viewed the F-82 Twin Mustang's use in Korea as a quick fix to supplement the limited number of short-range fighters available during the opening days of the conflict. However, it's operational commander, General Crabbe, had no intention of sacrificing the limited number of F-82G night fighters at his disposal over Korea for no clear purpose as they were also needed to cover mainland Japan and Okinawa against possible attack by the Soviets or Chinese. He reached this decision following the loss of five aircraft along with four crewmen between 29 June and July 6.

When F-82 production ceased in 1948, neither the Air Force nor North American had made any long-term provisions for stocking an adequate supply of

**F-82G named 'Dottie Mae' was operated first by the 4th F(AW)S before the 68th F(AW)S obtained it in December 1950. It went missing in action along with it crew Captain Julius C. Fluhr Jr, and Second Lieutenant Frederick Milhaupt Jr, on 14 March 1951. (*Robert F. Dorr*)**

**Sign for 339th F(AW)S Headquarters shows the Squadron emblem of a gremlin holding a bomb and riding a twin-headed eagle symbolic of the Twin Mustang. (*339th FIS Association via SMSgt. Bruce Campbell, USAF*)**

spare parts since both envisioned the aircraft would be out of front-line service by early-1950. The Air Force pulled the F-82E from its active inventory and most were in the process of being scrapped leaving only 168 F, G, and H Twin Mustangs to fulfil night fighting operations both in Korea, Japan, Okinawa, and the continental United States. Therefore, General Crabbe had no choice but to realign his night fighter assets and, within two weeks of the opening shots of the conflict, he pulled two of the three squadrons from Korean duty – the 4th and 339th F(AW)S. The 339th reduced its combat role on 5 July prior to returning to Japan to provide air defence from Itazuke Airbase, while the 4th F(AW)S returned to Naha, Okinawa on 8 July 1950. Both squadrons continued to play a reduced role in the Korean War when called upon by providing aircraft and crews to support the 68th 'Lightning Lancers'. Thus, the 68th F(AW)S became the only F-82 squadron to continue combat operations over Korea for a significant period of time.

The U.S. Eighth Army supported by a U.S. Marine Corps Brigade and ROK forces battled the NKPA through July and into September finally crushing North Korean opposition in September 1950 with U.S. forces landing at Inchon while the Eighth Army and supporting forces moved northward from Pusan. During July 1950, FEAF

F-82G, serial number 46-395, was better known as 'The Beast of the Far East' during its service with the 339th F(AW)S in Japan *circa* 1950. Nose art lettering was applied to both fuselages. The 4th F(AW)S acquired this aircraft in June 1950 operating it for a year until June 1951 when it was sent to Alaska for service with the 449th F(AW)S. (*339th FIS Association via SMSgt. Bruce Campbell, USAF*)

Another view of 'The Beast of the Far East' parked alongside another F-82G at Misawa Air Base, Japan *circa* 1950. The name is painted overall yellow. (*339th FIS Association via SMSgt. Bruce Campbell, USAF*)

used the 68th for close air support operations in Korea and during one, a joint effort conducted by B-26s, F-80s and F-82s on 10 July 1950, the Twin Mustangs contributed to the destruction of 117 trucks, 38 tanks, seven half-tracks, and caused an unknown number of North Korean casualties. Additional day strikes by F-82s ended the following day since FEAF did not want to expose the limited number of night fighters to enemy ground fire, but night close-air and interdiction strikes continued through August and September with the 'Lightning Lancers' conducting two notable air support missions on 25 and 30 August. Newly promoted Captain 'Skeeter' Hudson with radar operator Lieutenant Carl Fraser joined Lieutenant George Broughton and radar operator Master Sergeant Milton Griffin on a two-plane night close air support mission on 25 August when a U.S. Army unit came under intense mortar fire from a piece of South Korean territory known as Hill 409. Ground control guided the two F-82s through rain showers to enemy positions situated on the crest of the hill where they dropped 500lb bombs while unleashing withering HVAR rocket and machine gun fire. The American troops received no additional enemy fire after the aircraft departed and when the hill was taken unopposed the following day the soldiers counted more than 300 North Koreans dead – a testimony to the F-82's lethal arsenal. Five days later two night interdiction strikes disrupted the enemy's supply chain by hitting a railroad marshalling yard north of Seoul resulting in the destruction of three locomotives and numerous railway cars while a second strike by a pair of F-82s flown by First Lieutenant Ronald Adams, Jr, and First Lieutenant Robert Bolo lit up the night sky when they destroyed several trucks carrying ammunition. During August the squadron flew 125 sorties, destroying six locomotives, thirty-three boxcars, sixteen vehicles, and inflicted an indeterminate number of losses against NKPA ground troops.

General Partridge was impressed enough to commend the F-82 crews that participated in the mission for their skilful, aggressive, and determined action. It looked as if the 68th Squadron was bound to become one of the best USAF close air support and night interdiction squadrons of the Korean War. However, in September, the squadron went from being commended by FEAF and the Fifth Air Force for its operations in July and August, to being reprimanded, for gross negligence. The squadron's impressive debut over Korea with its two aerial victories on June 27 and subsequent air-to-ground attacks was overshadowed by two events that transpired on 11 September. On that day at 06.00 hours, a single F-82 flown by the 68th's commanding officer, Alden E. West, made four strafing passes against Taegu, South Korea, at that time held by American forces but which he mistook, in poor visibility, for the enemy-held town of Kunchon. One of the buildings hit by the Twin Mustang's machine gun fire happened to house the Fifth Air Force's

**An unidentified pilot, possibly Lieutenant Carboneau, according to the stencilled name, and his radar operator of the 339th F(AW)S aboard 'The Beast of the Far East' prepare to depart for combat air patrol from Japan. The two bars – one to the left of the wings below the canopy and the other to the left of the word 'The' – are painted red while the pilot's wings, wrench, and screwdriver shaft on the canopy frame are painted gray/silver, with the screwdriver's handle painted brown. (339th FIS Association via SMSgt. Bruce Campbell, USAF)**

**5-10: Captain William G. Hudson, in front of a 68th F(AW)S F-82G in December 1950. Hudson stands next to a line of five-inch HVAR rockets and a 500lb bomb prior to a ground support mission against Chinese Communists.** (*Warren Thompson via Robert F. Dorr*)

headquarters. General Partridge watched the attack from the steps of the building which resulted in the deaths of four South Koreans and the wounding of eight others. That mistake, along with the destruction of a badly needed bridge by a pair of 500lb bombs dropped from Lieutenant Robert Bobo's aircraft caused FEAF to take the squadron off combat duty and place it on a training status at Itazuke, Japan, for nearly two weeks. Partridge personally relieved West of his command with Captain James S. Alford Jr, taking temporary custody of the 68th until the arrival of Major 'Poke' Little, former commander of the 339th. Those two mistakes left the 68th's activities limited to flying weather reconnaissance missions over North Korea, in conjunction with a detachment of F-82s from the 4th F(AW)S.

The wife and children (Bill age 6 and Sharon age 5) of Captain Johnnie Gosnell, 68th F(AW)S, wave goodbye as he starts a mission in an F-82G based at Itazuke Air Base *circa* July 1950. Flight personnel conducted business eerily similar to a normal civilian job, getting up in the morning, going to work, and hopefully coming home at night to their families. Gosnell would return safely home to his family after this and many more missions over Korea. *(National Archives and Records Administration)*

An unidentified American airman conducting maintenance on the instrument panel of a 339th F(AW)S F-82G with the faded name 'Spring Fever' *circa* 1950. The names Lieutenant Walter Hayhurst, with pilot wings painted alongside, and crew chief Staff Sergeant Stephens with a screwdriver and crescent wrench, are written on the canopy frame. *(339th FIS Association via SM/Sgt. Bruce Campbell, USAF)*

Reconnaissance missions continued through the remaining months of 1950 consisting of one or two aircraft taking off from Itazuke between 01.00 and 02.00 hours. Such missions were long and laborious, lasting several hours, and without enemy contact as the North Korean Air Force had been wiped out and FEAF had turned night intruder work over to USAF B-26 intruder units. Maintenance personnel waged a war of their own trying to keep the 68th's Twin Mustangs airworthy as they could only keep three to four of the squadron's aircraft in commission at any one time between October and November. The squadron's total complement of aircraft had stood at nine during September with six considered combat ready, but the numbers were reduced to six with three airworthy by the end of November. The absence of the 4th and 339th F(AW)S, who needed their aircraft for long-range reconnaissance and air defence duties, left the 68th with a daunting task which forced them to cannibalize some F-82s in order to keep others in airworthy commission. It sharply reduced the number of sorties from 125 during August to thirty-one in October.

UN forces continued the ground and air offensive after the Inchon landing advancing into North Korea with the mission to destroy remaining NKPA forces and reunify Korea. However, Communist China's intervention on the side of North Korea at the beginning of November 1950 ended any such hope of reunification as Chinese Communist forces (CHICOM) pushed UN forces into full retreat. The first sign of Chinese intervention occurred during the early evening of 1 November when American soldiers of the Eighth Cavalry near Unsan, North Korea, experienced the full force of a CHICOM mass infantry assault; those that survived the ordeal were left stunned and shaken by the magnitude of the attack. This period of the conflict, known as the Chosin Reservoir Campaign, would be forever etched

Maintenance personnel at work on an unidentified 339th F(AW)S F-82G at Johnson Air Base, Japan, during 1950 with FQ-377 in the background. A lack of spare parts kept maintenance personnel extremely busy trying to keep the aircraft in operation. (*Author's Collection*)

Maintenance crew works on the engine of 'Lackin Blackin' of the 339th F(AW)S at Misawa Air Base, Japan in 1950. Note large circular inspection panels removed from the aft fuselage. The top of the vertical stabilizers are painted red. (*339th FIS Association via SMSgt. Bruce Campbell, USAF*)

Another F-82G that saw extensive service in the Korean War was 339th F(AW)S 'Gruesome Twosome' seen here at Misawa Air Base, Japan during the winter of 1950-51. The 68th F(AW)S obtained it in July 1951 from the 339th F(AW)S, remaining with that squadron until May 1952 when the 449th F(AW)S received it for use in Alaska. *(Author's Collection)*

Twin Mustangs prepare to depart from a snow-covered airbase in Japan for ground support strikes against enemy forces after Communist China's intervention in the Korean War. (*Author's Collection*)

into the memories of UN forces who fought in that bitter campaign that was characterized by extreme cold, hunger, and constant contact with overwhelming enemy forces. During November, Twin Mustangs of the 'Lightning Lancers' were pressed into flying an increasing number of reconnaissance sorties, supplemented

**The Far East Air Force's only fighter with night/all-weather capabilities from 1950 to mid-1951 was the F-82G Twin Mustang, a pair of which, including number twelve 'The Beast of the Far East' of the 339th F(AW)S, head out for combat air patrol over the Sea of Japan in deteriorating winter conditions. (*Author's Collection*)**

**The 339th F(AW)S was released from full combat operations over Korea on 6 July 1950 and returned to Japan; however, it continued to provide aircraft and crews to the 68th F(AW)S. (*Author's Collection*)**

by an occasional night interdiction mission or NCAP, accomplished by three serviceable aircraft.

The 4th F(AW)S provided a limited number of F-82s and crews beginning on 29 November to augment the 68th who, along with radar-equipped F4U-5N Corsairs and F7F-3N Tigercats of the Marine's VFW(N)-513 and -542, were providing night air defence of North Korea's capital of Pyongyang then, albeit briefly, under UN control. During December 1950 and January 1951 the 'Lightning Lancers' flew nearly 270 sorties. It was during an armed reconnaissance mission near Pyongyang on 27 January 1951 that Lieutenant Lawrence E. Anctil and his radar operator Lieutenant Robert L. Greer in F-82G serial number 46-399 disappeared.

The flight line at Itazuke Air Base, Japan, in 1950. The F-82G in the foreground belongs to the 68th F(AW)S and the Lockheed F-80 Shooting Stars are assigned to the 8th Fighter-Bomber Group. (*U.S. Air Force*)

A 339th F(AW)S Twin Mustang approaches Misawa Air Base, Japan from the east in 1950. (This base still exists today as a joint USAF/JASDF operation and is now home to F-16s and P-3s.) The 339th squadron was based there during 1950-51 before transferring to Johnson AFB at Imera, Japan. (*339th FIS Association via SMSgt. Bruce Campbell, USAF*)

*Below*: FQ-375, a 68th F(AW)S F-82G possibly seen at Itazuke Air Base in 1950 was lost in a non-fatal accident at P'ohang, South Korea on 7 December 1950. (*U.S. Air Force*)

# Chapter Six:
# Fade into History

UN forces retreated to the South, below the 38th Parallel. Thereafter, beginning in the spring of 1951, UN ground and air forces counterattacked forcing the Communists back to the imaginary line that divided the country. Afterwards, the conflict became a stalemate. In mid-1951, the 68th unit identifier, along with that of the 4th and 339th, changed from F(AW)S to Fighter Interceptor Squadron (FIS). The squadron began keeping a Twin Mustang on strip alert with F4U-5N Corsairs and F7F-3N Tigercats of the Marine's VMF(N)-513 and -542 in the Seoul-Souwon sector for night air defence against North Korean night hecklers called 'Bedcheck Charlies.' This arrangement seemed adequate in trying to knock down the slow-flying enemy observation aircraft until the appearance of Chinese MiGs over Seoul in early December 1951, which troubled General Otto Weyland, commanding officer of FEAF, and General Frank Everest, commanding officer of the Fifth Air Force. General Weyland voiced his concern to Washington by stating that the number of night fighters under his command was inadequate for the defence of Seoul, 'Present night fighters in Korea limited to six F-82s and a depleted squadron of Marine F7Fs.' Thus it was obvious to all concerned that propeller-driven F-82 (as well as F7F) night fighters were inferior in speed and would be no match against a MiG; therefore, having realized the obvious weakness in air defence, the USAF accelerated the conversion of the 68th and 339th Squadrons from the F-82 to the F-94 and committed the 319th FIS, the latter then based in the United States, for deployment to Japan for operations over Korea.

The 'Lightning Lancers' lost ten Twin Mustangs either through enemy action or from operational causes between 29 June 1950 and March 1951 reducing their complement of F-82s to five airworthy examples and the squadron remained at that strength through the early summer of 1951. Afterwards, the squadron limited combat use of its dwindling supply of aircraft. The F-82G officially left the Korean Theatre and FEAF in February 1952, and most were transferred to Tachikawa, Japan, where they were stripped of their black colouration, repainted a high-visibility red

FQ-400 an F-82G of the 68th F(AW)S crashed eighteen miles from base due to icing during a night reconnaissance mission on 7 December 1950 killing Captain Warren Harding and First Lieutenant Clifford Pratt. (*Author's Collection*)

F-82G 'Party Pooper' of the 339th and later the 68th F(AW)S had the name 'Our Lil' Lass' at one time. Note the top portion of this aircraft's stabilizer is painted red. (*339th FIS Association via SMSgt. Bruce Campbell, USAF*)

The same aircraft as the last photograph but with the name 'Our Lil' Lass' with in-squadron number three (instead of number two on 'Party Pooper') is shown here in Japan *circa* 1950-1951. This aircraft appears to have been surveyed as an operational loss at Suwon, South Korea on 6 November 1951. *(Norm Taylor Collection via Robert F. Dorr)*

**The last F-82G produced was 46-404 seen here with the 339th FIS at Johnson Air Base which transferred ownership to the 68th FIS in July 1951. Like many surviving Far East Air Force Twin Mustangs FQ-404 ended its service life with the 449th F(AW)S in Alaska. (*Author's Collection*)**

on the aft fuselage and outer wing panels, modified to F-82H configuration, and sent to the Alaskan Air Defense Command where they lived out their remaining service life. A few lingered on as target tugs with that Command until the last Twin Mustang on the Air Force roster, an F-82H, was retired by the Alaskan Air Defense Command on 12 November 1953, thus ending the aircraft's operational service.

During the Korean War, there was no real test of USAF night fighters against enemy aircraft during the first two years of the conflict; the three aerial victories scored by the F-82s occurred during the day. The reluctance to use that type of aircraft, due to shortage, combined with its inferior performance characteristics should it ever need to engage Soviet-built jet fighters precluded it from entering combat in areas where the opportunity for aerial engagement would have increased. In replacing Twin Mustang-equipped night fighter units in the Far East, the F-94 ran into three major problems regarding its use over the Korean Peninsula.

First, deployment of the Air Force's only jet-powered night fighter to Korea was delayed since the protection of North America from possible attack by nuclear-armed Soviet bombers flying in from Siberia took precedence, consequently, the F-94A/B went primarily to Air Defense Command in the continental United States and the Alaskan Air Command. Secondly, such aircraft were few in number with only 176 produced in FY 1951, and, therefore, the Air Force could only spare a limited quantity for the Korean conflict and so the first few F-94 interceptors only began arriving in Japan in March 1951. Finally, there was a highly sensitive issue regarding the jet's top secret Hughes E-1 Fire Control System. The Air Force assumed that hostile nations, meaning the Soviet Union and Communist China, would retrieve,

**A pair of 339th FIS F-82Gs prepares to depart from a snow-covered Misawa Air Base for a patrol along the east coast of Korea during 1951. The three Air Force all-weather F-82G squadrons were reclassified as Fighter Interceptor Squadrons (FIS) in mid-1951 as the squadrons transitioned to the Lockheed F-94. (U.S. Air Force)**

**The 68th FIS operated at least four F-82F Twin Mustangs (serial numbers 46-415, 418, 473, and 491) as the numbers of serviceable G models declined. Note single outer-wing bomb hard point. (*U.S. Air Force*)**

exploit, duplicate, and/or circumvent the system if an F-94 was ever lost over enemy-held territory in Korea. This last issue was the primary reason why the aircraft was not allowed to operate over North Korea for more than a year after arriving in the theatre. If F-94s had appeared earlier in the war, their presence may have resulted in a far superior number of aerial kills and, consequently, may have saved the lives of countless USAF bomber crews.

The Twin Mustangs served a small but important role with FEAF beginning with protecting the lives of American and South Korean evacuees at Inchon Harbor, Suwon, and Kimpo Airfield during the first tumultuous days of the Korean War. FEAF had no choice but to press their limited numbers of Twin Mustang night fighters since it was the only type of fighter capable of remaining on station for hours since the Air Force ruled out fuel-guzzling F-80 Shooting Stars based in Japan. However, by 1950 the aircraft was already obsolete and out-classed by both friendly and

**Captain Northcutt and Lieutenant Nichoalds standing in front of their F-82G served with the 68th FIS. They were some of the last in the squadron to fly the Twin Mustang until the unit transitioned to the Lockheed F-94B. (*Author's Collection*)**

hostile jet interceptors. North American Aviation's bold design for a high-performance long-range escort fighter for the B-29 bomber, presented to the USAAF during the last full year of the war in January 1944, ruled out the probability of it entering operational service in World War II. If the aircraft had been under development just a year earlier, and had become operational early enough to protect B-29 bombers against Japanese fighters, the F-82 Twin Mustang might have been remembered as one of the greatest American fighters in history.

The Twin Mustang fades into history. F-82G 'Dull Tool' is escorted by three of the U.S. Air Force's front-line jet fighters with its replacement the Lockheed F-94B all-weather fighter on its right wing, an F-80 on the left, with an F-86 behind. The Twin Mustang ended combat operations in the Korean Theatre with the 68th FIS in March 1952. (339th FIS Association via SMSgt. Bruce Campbell, USAF)

# Appendix A:
# P/F-82 Twin Mustang Specifications

## XP-82

**Dimensions**

Span: 51 feet 3 inches
Length: 39 feet 1 inches
Height: 13 feet 10 inches
Empty Weight: 13,402lbs
Gross Weight: 22,000lbs

**Performance**

Powerplant: two Packard Merlin V-1560-19/21
Maximum Speed: 468mph
Normal Range: 1,390 miles
Maximum Range: 2,600 miles (with external tanks)
Service Ceiling: 40,000 feet
Rate of Climb: 4,900 feet per minute

# P-82B

## Dimensions

Span: 51 feet 3 inches
Length: 38 feet 1 inches
Height: 13 feet 10 inches
Empty Weight: 13,405lbs
Gross Weight: 22,000lbs

## Armament

Six .50-caliber fixed machine guns (common to all production Twin Mustang variants)
Provision for additional eight .50-caliber pod-mounted machine guns housed in removable centreline pod
Four 1,000lb bombs
Two 2,000lb bombs
25-5in HVAR Rockets

## Performance

Powerplant: two Packard Merlin V-1560-19/21
Maximum Speed: 482mph
Normal Range: 1,390 miles
Maximum Range: 2,600 miles (with external tanks)
Service Ceiling: 41,600 feet
Rate of Climb: 4,900 feet per minute

# F-82E

## Dimensions

Span: 51 feet 3 inches
Length: 39 feet 11 inches
Height: 13 feet 10 inches
Empty Weight: 14,914lbs
Gross Weight: 24,864lbs

## Armament

As per the P-82B

## Performance

Powerplant: two Allison V-1710-143/1451
Maximum Speed: 465 mph
Maximum Range: 2,174 miles (with external tanks)
Service Ceiling: 38,400 feet
Rate of Climb: 4,020 feet per minute

# F-82F

## Dimensions

Span: 51 feet 6 inches
Length: 42 feet 2 inches
Height: 13 feet 10 inched
Empty Weight: 16,309lbs
Gross Weight: 26,208lbs

## Performance

Powerplant: two-Allison V-1710-143/145
Maximum Speed: 460mph
Cruising Speed: 280mph
Maximum Range: 2,400 miles
Service Ceiling: 38,500 feet
Rate of Climb: 3,690 feet per minute

## Armament (underwing stores)

2 2x 1,000lb Bombs
20-5in HVAR rockets

# F-82G and F-82H

## Dimensions

Span: Same
Length: 42 feet 5 inches
Height: Same
Empty Weight: 15,997lbs
Gross Weight: 25,891lbs

## Performance

Powerplant: Same
Maximum Speed: 460mph
Cruising Speed: Same
Maximum Range: 2,495 miles
Service Ceiling: 39,900 feet
Rate of Climb: 3,770 feet per minute

## Armament (underwing stores)

As per F-82F

# Major Avionics F-82F-H Series

## F-82F

AN/APG-28 Search and Tracking Radar.
SCR-695B IFF (also fitted to F-82E)
AN/ARN-5A and RC-103A Radio Receiving and Glide Path Set
AN/APS-13 Tail Warning Radar

## F-82G

Same as F-82F except for SCR-720 Radar

## F-82H

All of the above with the addition of: BC-453 and BC-454 low- and high-frequency radio receptor, AN/ART-13A long range liaison transmitter, plus winterization equipment.

# Appendix B:
# Korean War F-82G Twin Mustangs

| Serial | Unit | |
|--------|------|--|
| FQ-355 | 68th F(AW)S | |
| FQ-356 | 68th/339th/4th F(AW)S | 'Lackin Blackin' |
| FQ-357 | 68th F(AW)S | |
| FQ-358 | 4th F(AW)S | |
| FQ-359 | 4th F(AW)S | 'Misguided Virgin' |
| FQ-360 | 4th F(AW)S | |
| FQ-361 | 4th/68th/4th  F(AW)S | |
| FQ-362 | 4th F(AW)S | |
| FQ-363 | 68th F(AW)S | 'Siamese Lady' |
| FQ-364 | 68th F(AW)S | 'B.O. Plenty' |
| FQ-365 | 339th F(AW)S | |
| FQ-366 | 4th F(AW)S | |
| FQ-367 | 339th F(AW)S | 'Lover Boy' |
| FQ-368 | ? | |
| FQ-369 | 68th F(AW)S | 'Buzz' |
| FQ-370 | ? | |
| FQ-371 | 68th F(AW)S | 'Da Quake' |
| FQ-372 | 339th/68th F(AW)S | |
| FQ-373 | 68th F(AW)S | |
| FQ-374 | 68th F(AW)S | |
| FQ-375 | 68th F(AW)S | |

| | | |
|---|---|---|
| FQ-377 | 339th/4th F(AW)S | |
| FQ-378 | 68th F(AW)S | |
| FQ-379 | 339th/68th F(AW)S | 'The Dull Tool' |
| FQ-380 | 339th F(AW)S | |
| FQ-381 | 339th F(AW)S | 'Zero Zero' |
| FQ-382 | 4th F(AW)S | 'Night Takeoff' |
| FQ-383 | 68th F(AW)S | 'Bucket of Bolts' |
| FQ-384 | 4th F(AW)S | 'Wee Pea II' |
| FQ-390 | 4th F(AW)S | 'Midnight Sinner' |
| FQ-391 | 68th F(AW)S | |
| FQ-392 | 339th/68th F(AW)S | 'Party Pooper' and 'Our Lil' Lass' |
| FQ-393 | 68th F(AW)S | |
| FQ-394 | 4th/68th F(AW)S | 'Dottie Mae' |
| FQ-395 | 339th/4th F(AW)S | 'The Beast of the Far East' |
| FQ-396 | 68th F(AW)S | |
| FQ-397 | 4th/68th/4th F(AW)S | |
| FQ-398 | 339th F(AW)S | 'Black Jack' |
| FQ-399 | 68th F(AW)S | 'Doodle Bug' |
| FQ-400 | 4th/68th F(AW)S | 'Call Girl' |
| FQ-401 | 339th/68th F(AW)S | 'Gruesome Twosome' and 'Patches on the Patches' |
| FQ-402 | 4th F(AW)S | |
| FQ-403 | 4th F(AW)S | 'Miss Carriage' |
| FQ-404 | 339th/68th F(AW)S | 'Malfunction Junction' |
| FQ-415 | 68th F(AW)S | F-82F modified to F-82G |
| FQ-448 | 68th F(AW)S | F-82F modified to F-82G |
| FQ-473 | 68th F(AW)S | F-82F modified to F-82G |
| FQ-491 | 68th F(AW)S | F-82F modified to F-82G |

# Appendix C:
# Korean War F-82 Aircraft Losses

The following is a tabulation of Twin Mustangs and aircrews lost in the Korean theatre of operations beginning with date of loss, unit assignment, and circumstances surrounding the event. Data obtained from Korean War Aircraft Database (KORWALD).

| Date | Serial No | Unit | Circumstances |
|---|---|---|---|
| 28/06/50 | 46-358 | 339th F(AW)S | Crashed at Iwakuni while attempting to land. 2 killed |
| 06/07/50 | 46-402 | 68th F(AW)S | Crashed possibly near Chongmong-ni. 2 KIA |
| 07/08/50 | 46-355 | 68th F(AW)S | Lost southwest of Chinju-Sunchon. 2 KIA |
| 28/09/50 | 45-376 | | Mid-air collision with 16th FS F-80. 2 killed |
| 07/11//50 | 46-359 | 4th F(AW)S | Crashed into Naha Bay, Okinawa. 1 killed |
| 07/12/50 | 46-400 | 68th F(AW)S | Crashed 18 miles from base due to icing and loss of power during night weather recon mission. 2 KIA |
| 27/01/51 | 46-399 | 68th F(AW)S | Lost on combat patrol between Pyongyang and Kangdong. 2 MIA |
| 12/02/51 | 46-373 | 68th F(AW)S | Crashed during test northwest of Brady AFB, Japan. 1 killed |

| 14/03/51 | 46-394 | 68th F(AW)S | Lost on combat patrol between Seoul and Pyongyang. 2 KIA |
| 26/05/51 | 46-357 | 68th F(AW)S | Lost conducting weather recon north of 38th parallel. 2 MIA |

# Appendix D:
# Korean War F-82 Personnel Casualties

## 4th F(AW)S

| Date | Name | Status |
|------|------|--------|
| 06/07/50 | Fiebelkorn, Ernest C., Captain | KIA |
| 06/07/50 | Higgins, John J., First Lieutenant | KIA |
| 07/11/50 | Tymowicz, Adam P., Major | Non-battle death |

## 68th F(AWS/FI)S

| Date | Name | Status |
|------|------|--------|
| 12/07/50 | Harding, Warren G., Captain | KIA |
| 12/07/50 | Pratt, Clifford F., First Lieutenant | KIA |
| 07/08/50 | Meyer, Francis J., First Lieutenant | KIA |
| 07/08/50 | Moran, Charles B., First Lieutenant | KIA |
| 28/09/50 | Stanton, Billy D., First Lieutenant | KIA |
| 28/09/50 | McDonald, Robert., Captain | KIA |
| 07/12/50 | Harding, Warren., Captain | KIA |
| 07/12/50 | Pratt, Clifford., First Lieutenant | KIA |
| 27/01/51 | Anctil, Laurence A., Captain | MIA |
| 27/01/51 | Greer, Robert L., First Lieutenant | MIA |
| 12/02/51 | Boughton, George Jr., First Lieutenant | Non-battle death |
| 14/03/51 | Fluhr, Julius C Jr., Captain | MIA |
| 14/03/51 | Milhaupt, Frederick Jr., Second Lieutenant | MIA |

| 26/05/51 | Mulhallen, Ralph D., Captain | MIA |
| 26/05/51 | Nielsen, Arlid C., Captain | MIA |

## 339th F(AW)S

| Date | Name | Status |
| --- | --- | --- |
| 28/06/50 | Lindvig, Vernon A., First Lieutenant | KIA |
| 28/06/50 | Sayre, Derrell B., First Lieutenant | KIA |

# Appendix E:
# P/F-82 Unit Listing

**27th Fighter Escort Group**
522th Fighter Squadron
523th Fighter Squadron
524th Fighter Squadron

**52nd Fighter (All-Weather) Group**
2nd Fighter (All-Weather) Squadron
5th Fighter (All-Weather) Squadron

**84th Fighter (All-Weather) Wing**
496th Fighter (All-Weather) Squadron

**325th Fighter (All-Weather) Group**
317th Fighter (All-Weather) Squadron
318th Fighter (All-Weather) Squadron
319th Fighter (All-Weather) Squadron

**347th Fighter (All-Weather) Group**
4th Fighter (All-Weather) Squadron
68th Fighter (All-Weather) Squadron
339th Fighter (All-Weather) Squadron

**Alaskan Air Command**
449th Fighter (All-Weather) Squadron

**Note:**
*Some published sources have used unit designators FS(AW) for Fighter Squadron (All-Weather) and FG(AW) for Fighter Group (All-Weather) to identify such units.*

# Bibliography

## Books

Davis, Larry. *F-82 Twin Mustang*. Mini Number 8, Squadron/Signal Publications, Inc. Carrollton, TX, 1996.

McLaren, David R. *Double Trouble: P/F-82 Twin Mustang*. VIP Historical, Colorado Springs, CO, 1994.

## U.S. Government Sources

*Development of Night Air Operations 1941-1952*. Air Historical Studies No. 92, 1953.

Grant, C.L. *The Development of Continental Air Defense to 1 September 1954*. Air University USAF Historical Division Study1955.

Futrell, Robert Frank. *The United States Air Force in Korea, 1950-1953*.

Futrell, Robert F. *USAF Air Operations in the Korean Conflict (1 November 1950-June 1952), 1955*.

Knaack, Marcelle Size. *Encyclopedia of US Air Force Aircraft and Missile Systems Volume 1*. Office of Air Force History. Washington, D.C., 1978.

Thompson Wayne and Bernard C. Nalty. *Within Limits: The U.S. Air Force and the Korean War*. Air Force Historical Museums Program, 1996.

Y'Blood, William T. *MiG Alley: The Fight For Air Superiority*. Air Force History and Museums Program, 2000.

Stratemeyer, George E. *The three wars of Lt. Gen. George E. Stratemeyer: His Korean War Diary*. Edited by William T. Y'Blood.

*United States Air Force Operations in the Korean Conflict 25 June-November 1950*. USAF Historical Study No. 71, 1 July 1952.

# Periodicals

Grogan, Stanley J. Jr., Captain (USAF). *Lightning Lancers: Combat Highlights of the 68th Squadron in Korea.* The Airpower Historian Volume IX No. 4. October 1962.

Thompson, Warren. *Twin Mustang in Combat.* Flight Journal Volume 6, No 2, April 2001

Thompson, Warren. *Double Trouble: The North American F-82 in Korea.* Wings Magazine, Volume 13 No. 4., August 1983.

Thompson, Wayne and Bernard C. Nalty. *Within Limits: The U.S. Air Force and the Korean War.* Air Force History and Museums Program, 1996.

Trimble, Robert. *Twin Mustangs Part I.* Air Classics. Vol. 10, No. 3, March 1974

Trimble, Robert. *Twin Mustangs Part II.* Air Classics. Vol. 10, No. 4, April 1974

Sharp, John F., Colonel USAF (Ret.). *Flying the F-82 in Combat.* Pp. 49-57. Air Classics Vol. 10 No. 7. July 1974.

# Electronic Sources

Korean War Aircraft Database (KORWALD).
http://www.dtic.mi/dpmo/pmkor/korwald.htm

# GLOSSARY

| | |
|---|---|
| AAFB | Army Air Force Base |
| AFB | Air Force Base |
| CHICOM | Chinese Communist forces |
| CINCFE | Commander-in-Chief, Far East |
| F(AW)G | Fighter All-Weather Group |
| F(AW)S | Fighter All-Weather Squadron |
| FEAF | Far East Air Force |
| FEC | Far East Command |
| FEG | Fighter Escort Group |
| HVAR | High Velocity Aircraft Rockets |
| NAA | North American Aviation |
| NACA | National Advisory Committee for Aeronautics |
| NKPA | North Korean People's Army |
| ROK | Republic of South Korea |
| SAC | Strategic Air Command |
| USADC | U.S. Air Defense Command |
| USAF | U.S. Air Force |
| USAAF | U.S. Army Air Force |